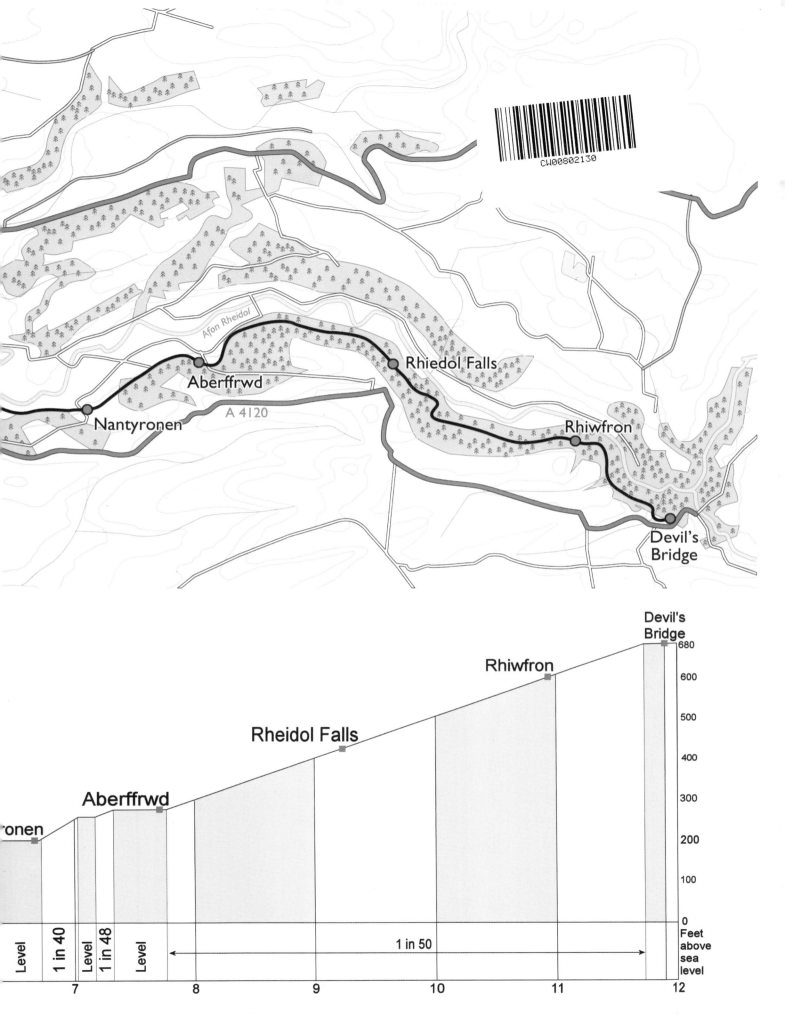

Nantyronen

Aberffrwd

A 4120

Afon Rheidol

Rhiedol Falls

Rhiwfron

Devil's
Bridge

Devil's
Bridge
680

Rhiwfron
600

500

Rheidol Falls
400

300

Aberffrwd

200

...ronen

100

0
Feet
above
sea
level

Level | 1 in 40 | Level | 1 in 48 | Level

1 in 50

7   8   9   10   11   12

THE VALE OF RHEIDOL RAILWAY

RAILWAY

THE STORY OF A NARROW GAUGE SURVIVOR

THE VALE OF RHEIDOL RAILWAY

THE STORY OF A NARROW GAUGE SURVIVOR

PETER JOHNSON

PEN & SWORD
TRANSPORT

AN IMPRINT OF PEN & SWORD BOOKS LTD
YORKSHIRE – PHILADELPHIA

FRONT COVER: No 1213 nears the end of another journey to Devil's Bridge. (John R. Jones)

BACK COVER:

UPPER: *Edward VII* at the first Aberystwyth station.

BACK COVER:

LOWER: 14 September 2019 was a great day for the railway, when its three GWR steam locomotives were lined up, in steam, in numerical order, in the same livery, for the first time.

ENDPAPERS: Plan by Gordon Rushton.

TITLE PAGE: The stunning scenery of the Rheidol valley is seen to perfection as No 8 climbs past Rheidol Falls. (John R. Jones).

First published in Great Britain in 2020 by
Pen and Sword Transport
An imprint of
Pen & Sword Books Ltd
Yorkshire - Philadelphia

Copyright © Peter Johnson, 2020

ISBN 978 1 52671 805 1

Typeset in Palatino 11/13 by Aura Technology and Software Services, India.

Printed and bound in India by Replika Press Pvt. Ltd.

Pen & Sword Books Ltd incorporates the Imprints of Pen & Sword Books Archaeology, Atlas, Aviation, Battleground, Discovery, Family History, History, Maritime, Military, Naval, Politics, Railways, Select, Transport, True Crime, Fiction, Frontline Books, Leo Cooper, Praetorian Press, Seaforth Publishing, Wharncliffe and White Owl.

For a complete list of Pen & Sword titles please contact

PEN & SWORD BOOKS LIMITED
47 Church Street, Barnsley, South Yorkshire, S70 2AS, England
E-mail: enquiries@pen-and-sword.co.uk
Website: www.pen-and-sword.co.uk

or

PEN AND SWORD BOOKS
1950 Lawrence Rd, Havertown, PA 19083, USA
E-mail: Uspen-and-sword@casematepublishers.com
Website: www.penandswordbooks.com

CONTENTS

ACKNOWLEDGEMENTS

I n July 1971 I made my first visit to the Vale of Rheidol Railway, and first to a Welsh narrow gauge railway, an event that turned out to be both life-changing and defining. In the following years I organised a rail tour excursion to Aberystwyth that included a chartered train on the railway for participants and arranged the first, and for many years the last, photo charter train, welcoming No 8 back to the railway following its overhaul at the Brecon Mountain Railway in 1996.

So it is with pleasure that I now devote a book to the railway. Some of the material was published in *An Illustrated History of the Great Western Narrow Gauge* (Oxford Publishing Co, 2011), which is now out of print. For that book I saw the 1897 Act of Parliament plans and the Great Western Railway's 1925 extension plans at the Parliamentary Archives, the company records and Cambrian Railways, GWR, British Railways, Board of Trade and Ministry of Transport files at the National Archives, Kew. To this I have added information from the Department of Transport's files dealing with the privatisation now accessible at the National Archives which include copies of the tenders, and a great deal of material obtained from digitised newspapers available online, the National Library of Wales's Welsh Newspapers Online collection (newspapers. library.wales) and the British Newspaper Archive (britishnewspaperarchive.co.uk). Reference was also made to *The Times* and *The Guardian's* digital archives and the *London Gazette* website. The timeline for events from the 1990s has been created from material that I contributed to my narrow gauge news columns in *Railway World* (1991-5) and *Steam Railway* (1995-2019) magazines.

Despite the increasing availability of cameras from the nineteenth century and the Vale of Rheidol Railway's location in a popular tourist location, there is a relatively small pool of images from which to draw for the first 50 years of the railway's existence. Even camera-owning railway enthusiasts rarely visited the line before the war. Having only six locomotives, five of one basic design and a visitor, and only two major stations, influences the range of images available too. Nevertheless, a number of 'new' images from this period have been uncovered. The situation changed post-war, but there were still events that received little photographic coverage. Even the change to private ownership in 1989 received scant attention – how could anyone tell the difference? Until the rolling stock was repainted there were few clues about the change in status. But slowly things changed and now there can be no doubt about the railway's independent status.

I would like to thank the railway's post-privatisation managers, Terry Turner, Neil Thompson and Llyr ap Iolo, for the warm welcome they and their staff have extended to me over the years, and the railway's chief executive, Rob Gambrill, for permission to make use of the railway's photo archives.

Michael Bishop, Alan Butcher, Adrian Gray, David Mitchell, John Scott Morgan and Dave Waldren (Cutting Edge Images) have kindly contributed photographs from their collections. Unfortunately the identities of many of the photographers are unknown but their names are given where possible. Unattributed photographs were either taken by me or are from my collection. Crown Copyright is reserved in images derived from Ordnance Survey mapping.

Responsibility for any errors or omissions must remain with me.

Peter Johnson
Leicester
October 2019

INTRODUCTION

I n 2018 the Vale of Rheidol Railway embarked on its biggest investment programme since it was opened in 1902. Over three years the passenger facilities at its main station, Aberystwyth, will be enhanced, a carriage shed constructed and the former GWR loco shed transformed into a multi-purpose space for displaying historic rolling stock and hiring out for functions, the result of nearly 30 years of hard work following the railway's privatisation in 1989.

From 1968 until 1989 the railway was the only steam line operated by British Rail, the nationalised railway operator. Inherited from the Great Western Railway upon Nationalisation in 1948, the 12-mile-long line was also the only narrow-gauge passenger railway under state control. By 1989 it was also run down and starved of investment.

With an Act of Parliament obtained in 1897, the railway's promoters had difficulty raising the funds needed to build it, and it was not opened until 1902. The engineer was James Weeks Szlumper, who had acted in the same capacity for proposed standard gauge branches to Devil's Bridge in the 1870s. The promoters were hoping to profit from the minerals to be found in the Rheidol valley as well as the tourists

attracted by the waterfalls and distinctive bridges that crossed one of them near the terminus.

The railway turned out not to be a great money spinner, but it made enough for its successive owners, the Cambrian Railways before the GWR and BR, to nurture it and to maintain its operations when other similar lines were closed. The GWR in particular invested in it, funding new locomotives, rolling stock and a station, and turned it into a seasonal tourist railway.

BR struggled to cope with the seasonal nature of its operations however, and a serious derailment in 1986 showed that its track maintenance left something to be desired. After a false start in the 1960s, in 1989 the railway became the first part of the nationalised railway to be privatised, coming under the control of a charitable trust which has directed its development since.

Under new management, a programme was started to restore the railway, infrastructure, rolling stock and facilities, to the highest standards. At the time of publication it is becoming clear that years of effort and investment are bearing fruit and that the railway is aiming to be among the front runners in the heritage railway industry.

CHAPTER 1

PLANNING, POWERS AND FUNDING

Without the railway, Aberystwyth would have been a typical Welsh west-coast market town with a small harbour. Even on modern roads with modern vehicles, the 75 miles to Shrewsbury or Swansea will take the better part of two hours to cover. The opening of the Aberystwyth & Welsh Coast Railway in 1864 brought access to markets that were not dependent on droving or the tides. It also brought tourists, and its existence must have contributed to the decision to found the University College Wales there in 1872.

Located where the confluence of the Ystwyth and Rheidol rivers encouraged the development of the harbour, evidence of human activity dating to the Mesolithic and the bronze and iron ages has been found in the area. Edward I's castle, built in 1277, was attacked by Parliamentarian troops in 1649, its ruins a local landmark. Development of the modern town followed the Local Government Act of 1887, which gave power to the electorate while removing it from landowners. Significant developments, the steam laundry, electric lighting, the pavilion and the Constitution Hill cliff lift, were the work of the Aberystwyth Improvement Company, an investment vehicle for the then Duke of Edinburgh, later the Duke of Saxe Coburg.

The railway takes its name from the Afon Rheidol, the larger of the two rivers. It rises on Plynlimon, the highest point in mid-Wales, some 19 miles to the north-east of the town, flowing southwards to Ponterwyd before narrowing into a ravine as it veers to the south-west and then westwards to join the Mynach at Pontarfynach, the bridge over the Mynach. The earliest reference to the Devil's Bridge appellation dates to 1734 and there is more than one legend to explain it.

Travellers to and from Aberystwyth were aware of the location's scenic attractions as it lay on the Llangurig to Aberystwyth turnpike. Never a village, nor even a hamlet, the only significant buildings were the Hafod estate's hunting lodge, the Hafod Arms Hotel since the 1820s, and the tollgate. There was only a small, scattered, community.

Two bridges crossing the Mynach gorge, one above the other, and a 300ft waterfall attracted tourists to the area, chief among them the artist J.M.W. Turner, in 1795, and the poet William Wordsworth, who was inspired to compose a sonnet about the experience in 1824.

The origins of the oldest bridge are unknown; it might have been built by the monks at the nearby Strata Florida abbey in the eleventh century. The second bridge was built in 1753 and iron railings were added in 1814. The former Cardiganshire County Council built the third to improve the road in 1901 and the original contractors strengthened it 70 years later. The bridges were listed in 1964.

In one sense the council's efforts were too late, because the turnpike had been diverted through Ponterwyd to Llanbadarn in the 1830s, the present A44, saving two miles, reducing the area's significance; the Devil's Bridge tollgate closed in 1845. However, the Cwm Rheidol lead mine, the largest and most productive in the area, and the needs of the Hafod estate, the principal landowner in the region, continued to give the area a purpose.

PONTERWYD ABERYSTWYTH

Industry in the Rheidol valley, the mill at Ponterwyd, with Plynlimon in the distance. Since replaced, the bridge carries the main A44 road from Llangurig to Aberystwyth.

PARSONS BRIDGE, ABERYSTWYTH.

Parson's Bridge, just over a mile upstream of Devil's Bridge, was another popular attraction for the 19th/early 20th century tourist. The Temple mine's 40ft waterwheel provided power for a crusher.

The bridges as they were when consideration was first given to promoting a railway to Devil's Bridge, before Cardiganshire County Council's road bridge was built in 1901. (Gyde's Photo Views)

Looking downstream from Rheidol Falls, with the famous stag created by the spoil from the Gellireirin lead mine on the opposite side of the valley. (Wrench)

With the Mynach falling through a 300ft waterfall to meet the Rheidol about ten miles from the coast, the valley opens out into good agricultural land, predominately grazing for sheep and cattle, the river meandering through a sparsely inhabited hinterland as it heads westwards.

The upper valley is littered with defunct mine workings, lead, zinc and copper amongst them, but, unlike many similar locations in Wales, no slate. Two-and-a-half miles downstream from Devil's Bridge, another, less substantial, waterfall lowers the level again, at the appropriately named Rheidol Falls. One landmark, visible for well over one hundred years, is the so-called Rheidol stag, the scar left by spoil dumped from mines at Gellireirin.

Twentieth century additions to the landscape are the Rheidol hydro-electric power station, opened in 1964 and the largest hydro station in Wales, and the planting of many of the upper slopes with conifers.

By the standards of the day, Aberystwyth was a boom town, with developments moving on apace. In 1855 *The Welshman* described it as a 'celebrated watering place

Rheidol Falls and Stag, Aberystwyth.

View in the Rheidol Valley, Aberystwyth.

A closer view of the miners' bridge across the river downstream of Rheidol Falls.

The Woodlands Bungalow was one of the catering establishments provided for tourists at Devil's Bridge. The building still exists, providing for users of a campsite. (Maglona Series)

TEA and LUNCHEON ALWAYS READY. REFRESHMENTS

ne Woodlands Bungalow, Devil's Bridge.

Development of Aberystwyth's Victoria Terrace was incomplete when this view of the town was taken. The ornate building at the far end of the promenade was built for the contractor Thomas Savin as a hotel but was incomplete when he entered bankruptcy in 1866 and sold to the University College of Wales at a considerable loss.

… filled with distinguished visitors.' Funds were being raised for the town clock and a daily omnibus conveyed visitors to the celebrated Devil's Bridge.

The first schemes to take a railway to or near Devil's Bridge were ancillary to proposals to create a through route between the North-West of England and the South-West of Wales. Both the North & South Wales Railway, which deposited a Bill for a railway between Llanidloes and Lampeter in 1853, and the Manchester & Milford Railway, which obtained an Act for its route between the Carmarthen & Cardigan Railway at Pencader and the Llanidloes & Newtown Railway at Llanidloes in 1860, would have passed through the Rheidol valley between Devil's Bridge and Ponterwyd.

The Manchester & Milford Railway then obtained powers for a branch to Aberystwyth from Devil's Bridge in 1861, which was abandoned within two years, and went on to obtain powers for a branch to Devil's Bridge from Crosswood in 1873. This scheme had replaced the independent Devil's Bridge Railway scheme on the same alignment, which had failed during the parliamentary process the year before; everything was perfect, reported the *Cambrian News* on 19 January 1872, until

the deposit was due to be paid; only two of the six directors attended a meeting to approve its payment and they received notice that three of their colleagues had resigned.

An advertisement for the Waterloo Hotel's 'posting branch', which offered a daily service to Devil's Bridge. Thomas Morris, the hotel's owner and coach operator, died on 12 November 1909, aged 79. The *Welsh Gazette*'s obituary of him gave an insight into Aberystwyth's transport links before the railways arrived, explaining that he had run a coach between Aberystwyth and Carmarthen until the Manchester & Milford Railway had opened, between Aberystwyth and Llanidloes until the Cambrian Railways connected those places, and then to Devil's Bridge until the railway opened, when he sold his charabancs. The hotel was demolished a few years ago.

An extract from the deposited plan for the Manchester & Milford Railway's proposed Aberystwyth–Devil's Bridge branch, with its triangular junction near Devil's Bridge. (Parliamentary Archives)

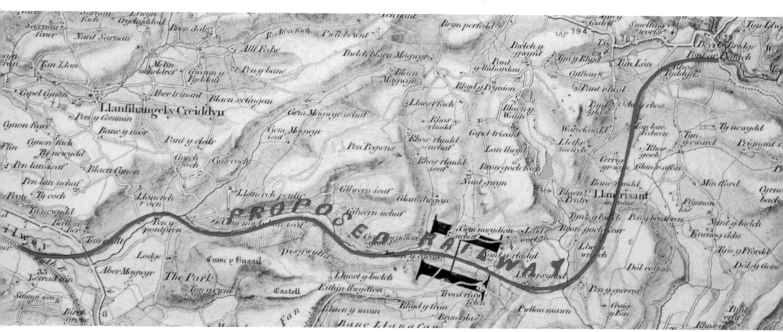

The plan deposited with the independent Devil's Bridge Railway Bill in 1871. Surveyed by James Weeks Szlumper, the same route was adopted by the Manchester & Milford Railway the following year. Both schemes failed. (Parliamentary Archives)

In 1895 the *Aberystwyth Observer* (21 November) said that a Captain Bray and others had paid over £100 for a survey to be made 'a quarter of a century ago', which must refer to the 1871/2 scheme. Nicholas Bray was a Cornish mining engineer and agent who owned a mine in, and lived in, Goginan.

All these schemes were for standard gauge lines. The engineer for both the 1872 and 1873 schemes was James Weeks Szlumper. In 1876 an extension of time to purchase the land required was obtained but in 1880 it was formally abandoned.

The next development in the advancement of a Devil's Bridge railway occurred during an auction of property belonging to the Nanteos estate in July 1892. A lot containing several properties in the Rheidol valley, including mineral rights, was one of the few that sold and both the auctioneer and the purchaser, a George Green, appeared to think that there was a likelihood of a railway being built that would benefit the property.

Green was a mining engineer born in Staffordshire who grew up in Manchester, where he received his training. Visiting Aberystwyth to erect a steam engine in the town's only foundry in 1848, he never left, establishing a business that supplied mining machinery around the world. He was also active in local politics, despite losing more elections than he won. In September 1892 he announced at the mayor's banquet that there was a movement to build a railway to Devil's Bridge that he hoped would be done before the start of the 1893 season.

He was soon to be disabused of that notion and it would be another 10 years before the railway was opened to the public. However, there had been some progress towards a railway to Devil's Bridge. On 19 December 1892, the *Evening Express* reported being told that J.W. Szlumper had surveyed the route for a narrow gauge line from Aberystwyth through the Rheidol valley earlier in the year. The money required, said the paper, was in place provided the landowners would donate their land.

However, on 3 February 1893, the *Cambrian News* reported that land negotiations were 'pending', adding that landowners were 'considering the matter in a reasonable way', implying that they would recognise the public benefit of a railway and be generous when making their land available for it. The question of land value was one that would surface several times before the railway was built, particularly in Aberystwyth. There it was thought that the Cambrian Railways had benefitted unduly by the uplift in land values since land had been bought from the fledgling council for the Aberystwyth & Welsh Coast Railway in the 1860s, not realising that without the railway the land would not have increased in value.

Meeting on 20 June 1893, the town council passed a resolution in support of the railway, debating whether or not to release land at a nominal value or fair rent. One councillor pointed out that if the railway took the land from the harbour and along the river and built an embankment on it, it would save the council the cost of doing so itself. Another did not vote because he felt they had insufficient information about the proposal.

At the next meeting, on 4 July, Green proposed a motion committing the council to releasing land for the railway at a nominal rent but agreed to a proposal to refer it to a committee instead. The *Aberystwyth Observer* saw this as the final blow to the scheme, forecasting that it would not be revived for 'many years to come', saying that the land concerned was 'absolutely valueless'.

There was no more activity recorded and Green died in March 1895, his vision for a railway up the Rheidol valley unfulfilled. However, a month before his death the Royal Commission on Land in Wales and Monmouthshire, meeting in London, heard evidence in favour of local authorities participating in the promotion of light railways to improve access to rural areas. H. Enfield Taylor of Chester reeled off a long list of places that he thought would benefit, including 'from Aberystwyth, up the valley of the Rheidol, to the foot of the falls at the Devil's Bridge, with a lift for passengers and goods to the summit, and a branch to the great district centring on Goginau'. The last is now known as Goginan, and the Ordnance Survey has recorded many disused mines in its vicinity.

This initiative would have been in support of the Light Railways Bill which was enacted on 14 August 1896. Intended to encourage the development of remote areas, the legislation provided for the creation of a commission that would put it into effect. It authorised local authorities and others to apply for powers to build railways, permitted local authorities to make loans to, or invest in, such railways, and allowed the treasury to make advances not exceeding a quarter of the capital.

Light railways would be freed of the requirements, sometimes onerous and expensive, placed on main line railways by the Board of Trade, which imposed the requirements of the Railway Clauses Consolidation Act 1845 and other legislation to all railways regardless of whether they were carrying thousands of passengers a day or a few dozen. With recommendations by the commission and confirmation by the Board of Trade, Light Railway Orders when made would have the same status as if enacted in Parliament. The process was expected to be considerably cheaper too.

Had they been prepared to wait for a few months, the Vale of Rheidol Railway promoters, mine owners, the Hafod estate, some farmers, and others who were interested in the development of Aberystwyth generally, could have taken advantage of the new legislation. However, on 15 November 1895 advertisements announced their intention to deposit a Bill in Parliament.

Two 2ft gauge railways were proposed, No 1 from the north-eastern corner of enclosure No 72 abutting Smithfield Road in Aberystwyth and terminating at the eastern boundary of enclosure No 98 in the parish of Upper Llanfihangel y Creuddyn, Devil's Bridge. Railway No 2 commenced at the southern end of the quay of Aberystwyth harbour and terminated at a junction with railway No 1 at the north-western corner of enclosure No 73.

'It is intended,' stated the notice, 'to work the aforesaid railway as a light railway and to apply the provisions … of the Regulation of Railways Act 1868 … as to the crossing of roads on the level, limiting the speed of engines, and otherwise in such manner as the bill may prescribe.'

The 1868 Act empowered the Board of Trade to issue a licence authorising the construction and operation of a railway as a light railway providing axle loads did not exceed eight tons and speed did not exceed 25mph. The Board remained reluctant to relax the 1845 standards and little use was made of the 1868 legislation. One of the issues remained the expense of obtaining compulsory purchase powers despite

The deposited plan for the Vale of Rheidol Railway's Act of Parliament. (Parliamentary Archives)

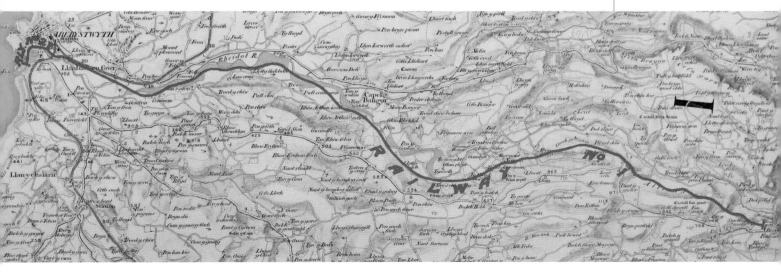

attempts to reduce costs by introducing simplified procedures in 1864 and 1870.

The Bill's local solicitor was Arthur J. Hughes, who was also the town clerk and who did much to promote the railway's cause. The engineer was J.W. Szlumper who had surveyed the route to Devil's Bridge for the 1870s standard gauge schemes. Born in London in 1834, his father was a tailor born in an area with fluid borders, changing from German to Polish control, which affected the answer he gave to the question about his birthplace to census enumerators. His mother was English. The family later moved to Pembrokeshire, where Szlumper started his civil engineering career.

Engineer Hamilton H. Fulton recruited him as an assistant circa 1853. After six years in Fulton's office he was resident engineer of the Milford (Haven) Railway, the Stoke's Bay Railway & Pier and the Manchester & Milford Railway, before working on the Barry Railway, the Vale of Glamorgan Railway, the Cardiff-Ogmore line, and the Pontypridd, Caerphilly & Newport Railway, the Isle of Wight Railway (eastern section), the Brompton & Piccadilly Railway, the North Wales Narrow Gauge Railways and the Lynton & Barnstaple Railway.

Becoming established, he set up homes in Aberystwyth and Kew Gardens, becoming prominent in civic affairs in both locations. In Cardiganshire he was appointed county surveyor in 1864, a magistrate in 1887, High Sheriff in 1897 and Deputy Lieutenant in 1898. In Richmond he was appointed a magistrate in 1893, when he also became the borough's first mayor, holding that office three times. He was knighted in 1894.

The Rheidol Bill was postponed, due to insufficient time according to the *Cambrian News* on 1 May 1896, which at the same time erroneously forecasted that the forthcoming Light Railways Act would be used to secure the necessary powers.

In August the *Aberystwyth Observer* thought the project had been abandoned, but a month later reported that it had been reactivated. But on 19 November it complained about the route to be taken

east of Llanbadarn, saying that it would be better if it ran to the north of the river where there were several large houses and the population was higher. If the promoters persisted with the route south of the river, it said, then there would be some advantage to having a branch line serving Capel Bangor. A week later it said that the valley's inhabitants were saying that they would prefer the scheme to be abandoned, hoping that someone else would take it up and modify the route, and were threatening to oppose the bill if it proceeded without change.

Despite this intervention, the Parliamentary notice published on 10 November maintained the route to the south of the river. At a public meeting held in Aberystwyth on 2 December, Szlumper explained that it was essential for the terminus to be near the hotel to facilitate any future extension and that the cost of crossing the ravine prevented a route north of the river being adopted. His explanation though did not prevent Melindwr parish council from continuing to push for a northern route, preferring, it said, not to oppose the Bill in parliament. In January 1897, Szlumper offered to provide a branch to Goginan provided the land was made available at agricultural values, a promise that he was not called upon to fulfil.

The offer though obviously neutered the parish council's threat, for the Bill went through Parliament unopposed. There was a problem however with the route proposed for the harbour branch crossing the foreshore at Aberystwyth. Taking the shortest route around the harbour, Szlumper intended to close a 60ft gap in the harbour wall, not taking into account that the ground beyond was used by fishermen to beach and maintain their boats.

The Board of Trade, exercising powers given to it by the Preliminary Inquiries Act of 1851 and the Harbours Transfers Act of 1862, appointed vice-admiral Sir George Strong Nares KBC, FRS to inquire into the likely effects on navigation. He conducted his inquiry in the town hall on 3 March.

The fishermen's representative claimed that closing the gap would deny them from using the only safe mooring in the harbour. Evidence was given that harbour use was in decline, 395 vessels had used it in 1861, but only 40 after the Aberystwyth & Welsh Coast Railway had opened in 1864, the shipbuilders relocating to Porthmadog.

With Sir George recommending that the gap should not be closed, Szlumper informed the *Cambrian News* that he had met him and the assistant secretary to the Board of Trade on 9 March 1897 and reached agreement for routing the railway past the area, just below the high-water mark. The proposal to close the gap appears to have been made in consultation with the council. The Board of Trade recommended to Parliament that the railway should be diverted, or if the route on the deposited plan was adhered to then a bridge with an opening span should be constructed.

Local newspapers reported the Bill's passage through Parliament with increasing excitement. On 15 April the *Aberystwyth Observer* reported that Szlumper was accustomed to executing heavy works in the most expeditious manner, adding that it understood that the railway would be ready for the summer of 1898. Two days later, the *Montgomery County Times* claimed that trains would be running every 30 minutes during the summer, a feat that would have required more than double the rolling stock with which the railway was equipped.

An aerial view of Aberystwyth c1950, with the route of the harbour branch highlighted. The gap in the harbour wall is clearly visible.

The Act received the royal assent on 6 August 1897. The Vale of Rheidol (Light) Railway Company was incorporated. The gauge could be increased up to 4ft 8½in at any time with the prior approval of the Board of Trade. The capital was £39,000. Three bridges over public roads were sanctioned, at Llanbadarn, Nantyronen and Aberffrwd. Three years were allowed to exercise the compulsory purchase provisions and five years for construction. The promoters were John Francis, Walter Taylor and Hugh Lowe. The first had been born in Llanbrynmair in 1837 and was a businessman, owning a chain of grocery shops in the London area. Locally, he owned the Wallog estate, enlarged to 700 acres since he had bought it, to the north of Aberystwyth. The identities of the other two have not been established; their involvement was to be brief. Joining Szlumper as engineer was William Weeks Szlumper, his brother. Both had signed the estimate for £32,000.

Capital for the new line was hard to come by so it might be relevant that within a short time the light railway legislation had been invoked to obtain an order for an extension, in reality a branch, 16½ miles to the coastal town of Aberayron,

Aberaeron in Welsh. The public notice for the application was published on 8 October 1897. The extension would share the Vale of Rheidol Railway's Aberystwyth terminus, diverging from it close to the point where it was intended to pass under the Manchester & Milford Railway.

Reviewing the application, the light railway commissioners deplored the use of the 'very small gauge' – there was no need for it as the railway was routed on its own land and not in the road. The 2ft 6in gauge line from Welshpool to Llanfair had been sanctioned, 'and if this gauge could be adhered to for the hilly parts of Wales, some of them may perhaps be connected with one another hereafter, and then it would be a great advantage if they were all of the same gauge… If the conditions of the already sanctioned Vale of Rheidol Light Railway are similar … it would be a great improvement to construct both lines with a gauge of 2ft 6in instead of 2ft.'

The commissioners noted a curious feature in the draft order concerning the capital and revenue. The Aberaeron capital and Devil's Bridge capital were to be kept separate but their revenues and expenses would be pooled. The net revenue would then be shared, not in proportion of capital

Aberaeron at the turn of the twentieth century. (Davies)

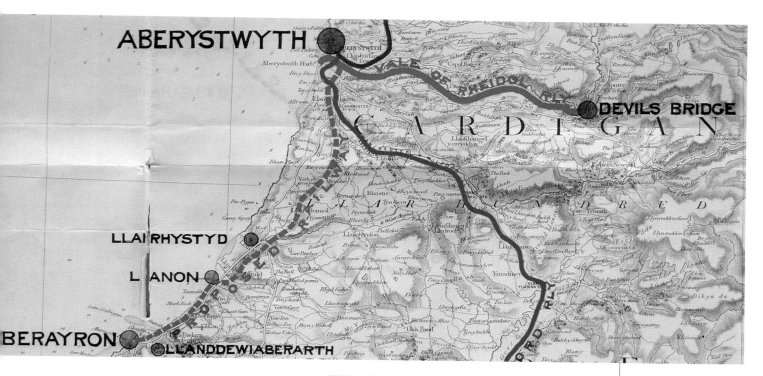

ABERYSTWYTH

DEVILS BRIDGE

CARDIGAN

LLAIRHYSTYD

LLANON

BERAYRON

LLANDDEWIABERARTH

but in proportion to the lengths of the two lines, with the result that the shareholders of the line constructed more cheaply would get a better return. They thought the estimate of £54,567 was high 'for a line of this very small gauge'.

They concluded their review with the observation that the proposal was probably not the best way of serving the area. The first four miles duplicated the Manchester & Milford Railway's route from Aberystwyth. A junction at this point would save four miles and the remaining 12 miles could probably be built for the same amount as the current proposal 'and in this way the district would get a standard gauge line at about the same cost as a miserable little 2ft gauge line.'

The Manchester & Milford Railway did, of course, object on the grounds that the proposal was unnecessary, competitive, and would cause loss and injury to it. Nevertheless, following an inquiry in Aberystwyth on 4 April the Vale of Rheidol Light Railway (Aberayron Extension) Order was made on 13 August 1898. The company was to keep separate accounts for the extension.

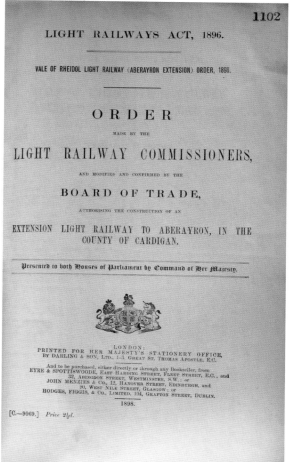

Extract from the deposited plan for the Vale of Rheidol Light Railway (Aberayron Extension) Order application. (National Archives)

The extension light railway order.

Construction of a standard gauge railway proposed in 1897 might have had some impact on the Vale of Rheidol Railway had it been built. First mooted in 1893, the East & West Wales Railway's Bill was deposited at the same time as the Aberaeron extension application was made, and proposed a route connecting the Manchester & Milford Railway at Llanilar with the Mid-Wales Railway at Rhayader and the Kington & Eardisley Railway at New Radnor that would have passed close to Devil's Bridge.

Promoted by the Aberystwyth Improvement Company, the estimates were signed by George Croydon Marks, the engineer who had built the Constitution Hill cliff railway in 1895/6, and Ridley Henderson. The Bill failed when the Parliamentary committee was not persuaded that sufficient funds were available to complete the 50-mile railway. A second attempt a year later collapsed when the promoters failed to attend Parliament to support the Bill in accordance with standing orders. The days of raising capital,

£700,000 in this case, for standard gauge railways in mountainous areas of Wales were clearly over. Marks, who was later ennobled, also built the cliff railways at Lynton, Bridgnorth and Clifton, the cable tramway at Matlock and the Pier Pavilion and Hotel Cambria in Aberystwyth.

There had been little progress on the Devil's Bridge line beyond discussions with the town council concerning the land required for the station. On 10 February 1898 the *Aberystwyth Observer* reported that there were still landlords unwilling to release their land at agricultural values, preferring to go to arbitration and increase the railway's expenses to an extent that exceeded the land's value.

A week later the paper had heard from two of them. 'I simply want a fair price,' John Bonsall had said. 'I have children and must think of them. I cannot give the land for nothing.' The paper responded with mock sympathy, quite unusual at a time when the lower orders were still expected to defer to the upper classes. 'As Mr Bonsall is one of the wealthiest

An extract from the plan deposited with the Bill for the South & West Wales Railway in 1899, showing the proximity of the proposed route to Devil's Bridge. (Parliamentary Archives)

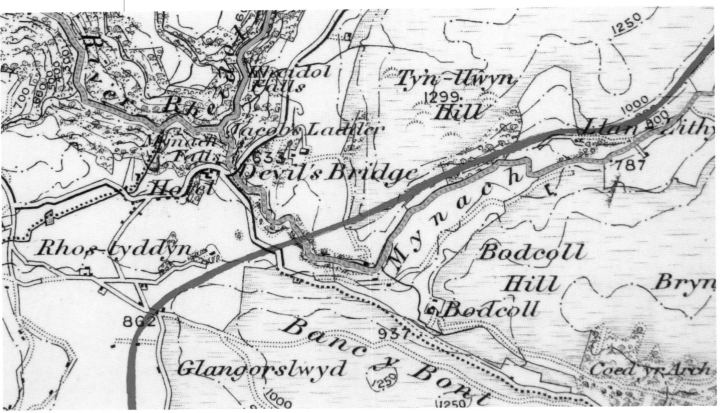

men in the country we could not help sympathising with him, especially in the difficulty he experiences in laying out his money, and we told him that if we have a half-penny to spare when the time of adversity comes we will share it with him, a promise which comforted him greatly.'

In July the town clerk informed the council that capital to build the railway was available providing the land could be obtained at agricultural valuation, but as the *Aberystwyth Observer* reported that the landowners were starting to come round to the railway's point of view, it also reported that some councillors were saying that they thought the council land should be sold for as much as £40 an acre, contrasting it with a deal done for the recreation ground at £1 an acre.

The council dealt with Szlumper's offer on 19 July. The railway had, he wrote, reduced its land take for the station site to just over two acres and was prepared to pay no more than £800 for that, the strip along the river bank and the strip of rough ground at Plascrug. He also offered to pay 4% interest from the commencement of

work until the conveyance was completed, an offer which was to consume the councillors' time for several years. The offer was more than the railway had wished to pay, Szlumper continued, threatening to abandon the railway if satisfactory terms could not be agreed.

The councillors were divided on whether to stick out for £15 an acre, £862 10s, or push for £17. After an extensive debate, during which the mayor refused to put the motion to sell the land without the prior approval of the Local Government Board, a motion to insist on £15 an acre was lost in favour of accepting Szlumper's offer, subject to the Local Government Board's approval. The board exercised oversight of local authorities from 1871 until 1919. Among its responsibilities it had to approve the disposal of assets.

Despite the council's decision on the land, there was still no progress towards building the railway. On 16 March 1899 the *Aberystwyth Observer* noted that nothing had been heard of the railway for some time and feared that the scheme had been

J.W. Szlumper's plan showing the land acquired from Aberystwyth Town Council for part of the harbour branch, the station and loco shed and the strip at Llanbadarn. (National Archives)

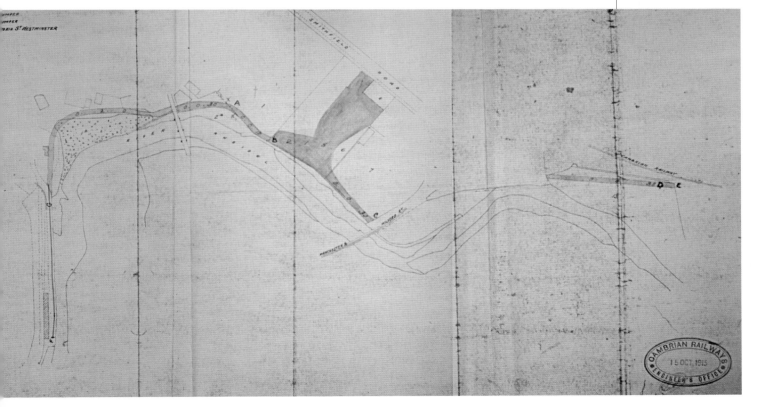

ended, forecasting that a new generation would revive it in 30- or 50-years' time.

The next development came on 10 November 1899, when the company announced that it would seek further powers in Parliament, notably extensions of time for compulsory purchase of land and to complete the 1897 works, and to work both the Devil's Bridge and Aberaeron lines by electricity. Without meeting any objections, the second Vale of Rheidol Light Railway Act gained the royal assent on 30 July 1900. Two years were given to purchase land and the time to complete the Devil's Bridge line was extended by three years, to 1905. £12,000 of new capital and borrowing powers for £4,000 were also sanctioned.

This was enough to get things started, but not before the *Aberystwyth Observer* commented (29 November 1900) that nothing had been heard either of the Devil's Bridge or the Aberayron schemes for some time and that it was 'just possible that they are both virtually dead'.

On 20 December 1900 however, the *Welsh Gazette* was able to report that 'several influential gentlemen' had visited the neighbourhood in connection with the scheme, that finance was in place and that the landowners were 'willing to compromise the difference that hitherto existed'.

The directors met for the first time on 10 January 1901. The board comprised the promoters Francis, Taylor and Lowe, together with Henry Herbert Montague Smith and W.T. Madge. The last two appear to have been appointed just before the meeting started; both had London addresses. Taylor and Lowe were not at the meeting and the latter's resignation was dealt with during it, when he was replaced by Robert William English Parker. Smith was elected chairman. Born in 1858, his father, William Smith, was a civil engineer. The *Aberystwyth Observer* (13 November 1902) said that Smith had been involved in the promotion of the City & South London and Central London railways, the first deep tubes on the London underground system.

If that was the case then he was almost certainly acquainted with Szlumper, whose personal firm was engaged on aspects of the Great Northern, Piccadilly & Brompton Railway, a constituent of the Piccadilly Line of London's underground railways. A 1903 *Railway News* article said that the promoters had approached Smith to use his contacts to move the project forward.

The Szlumpers, present at the meeting, were appointed the company's engineers and a draft agreement with them approved. A. J. Hughes, the town clerk, also present, was appointed local solicitor with an obligation to conduct negotiations for the land required, acting for the company locally until the railway was opened and paying survey fees, for £250. He was to 'take all necessary steps' to acquire the land needed 'without delay'.

Smith reported that he was authorised to apply for 350 £10 shares on behalf of Works Syndicate Limited, paying for the shares in full provided that one other director nominated by the syndicate in addition to himself was elected to the board, that Lumley & Lumley be appointed the company's London solicitors, and that the syndicate have first call on any debentures issued.

The syndicate had been registered for the purpose of raising capital for new developments in 1891. With Smith abstaining, his proposal was accepted. Parker, a contractor, was the other syndicate nominee. Syndicate shareholders included Sir Douglas and Francis Fox and James Henry Greathead, the civil engineers. The choice of solicitor is explained by the £3,000 investment registered to Walter Lumley. By 1897 the syndicate had raised £7,006 capital. Nothing is known of any other investments.

Other shares were allocated thus: 325 to Smith, 20 each to Francis, Taylor, Lowe, Parker, Madge and Hughes, 20 to J.W. Szlumper and 10 to W.W. Szlumper, including the syndicate's 350, a total of £8,250.

Having released the syndicate's £3,500, payments had been approved: £1,552 10s

10d to Hughes for expenses in connection with the Act and the order; £900 to W.W. Szlumper for costs incurred to date; £990 to W. William Bell, parliamentary agent's charges for Act and order; and £10 to petty cash, total £3,452 10s 10d. It is likely that the holders of the non-syndicate shares had only paid a nominal deposit for them at this date.

John Richard (1853-1922) and Arthur Henry Pethick (1856-1934) were also present at the meeting, representing their Plymouth-based family firm, Pethick Brothers. Their tender of 21 December 1900 was read and Smith and the Szlumpers were deputed to arrange terms with them. The other brothers were Benjamin Herbert (1860-1943) and Nicholas Frank (1863-1926). Contractors of some standing, capable of taking on very large contracts ranging from mansions to public works,

the firm's activities were overseen by the brothers' father, John Pethick (1829-1904), who had started as a builder and contractor in 1852.

Among other works, they built the Vale of Glamorgan Railway, were responsible for widening the old London Bridge, and rebuilding Vauxhall Bridge. In his 1943 paper about the railway (see Bibliography), James Rees, who became its manager, said that the Pethicks became interested in the contract because they had no use for the rail released by the completion of their Bristol water works contract, which rather sounds like the tail wagging the dog.

The final matter dealt with on 10 January 1901 was the parliamentary deposit, £1,560, paid by the promoters. The directors resolved to secure its release, free of deductions and with interest, in order that it could be repaid as soon as possible.

Rheidol Falls.

Some 250ft below the railway, the Rheidol falls were a greater attraction in Victorian times than they are in the 21st Century.

CHAPTER 2
CONSTRUCTION

When the town council met on 11 January 1901, A.J. Hughes, town clerk and solicitor, briefed it about the railway, saying that all the capital had been applied for and allotted, which does not accord with what he had just recorded in the company's minute book. On the company's behalf and as a gesture of goodwill he offered to pay a deposit in excess of the usual 10% for the council's land. To speed the work, he added, construction would start from both ends at the same time.

On 24 January the *Western Gazette* reported good progress being made with land owners, such that it anticipated that the company would not have to use its compulsory purchase powers. It also reported that in addition to the terminals there would be stations at Llanbadarn, Rhiwarthen and Tyllwyd, near Aberffrwd. Rhiwarthen was known as Capel Bangor from the railway's opening.

Meeting next on 15 February, the directors allocated shares totalling £4,560, with the four Pethick brothers taking 1,125 each. Lowe's shares were transferred to Charles E. Cottier, Pethick Brothers' solicitor.

Pethick Brothers' tender to build the railway for £45,000 was accepted and the contract was signed on the same date. The shares they had agreed to take were therefore 10% of the contract price. They would anticipate selling them at a profit when the railway was completed. A separate item allowed the Pethick brothers to use second-hand rail already in stock providing it weighed more than the 42lbs/yard specified.

At the company's first general meeting held on 28 February, A.H. Pethick and W.W. Szlumper took the opportunity to put their stamp on the board, opposing Parker's re-election by nominating Francis (Frank) Joslin Ellis, an estate agent and member of Plymouth Town Council, instead. Parker was ejected with five votes against and only one in favour. Cottier was also elected a director. Judged by his regular attendance at meetings, W.W. Szlumper appears to have been more actively engaged in the construction than his brother, perhaps because the latter was occupied by his concurrent position as the Brompton & Piccadilly Railway's engineer.

When the council met on 5 February, it gave permission for the company to take possession of its land provided a £400 deposit was placed in the joint names of the company and the town council. It also required £1 1s annually for the easement permitting rails to be laid to Rofawr wharf, specifying that if the railway there ceased to be used for a period of one year the easement would cease and be determined. Hughes reported that the contractors were in the town making arrangements to start work.

On 25 February Aberystwyth Rural District Council considered and approved the company's request to cross five roads on the level instead of by bridge as legislated. The company undertook to install cattle grids instead of gates.

Work was started without ceremony on an unrecorded date. On 19 March Hughes told the council that the company had paid the 50% deposit, which entitled it to take possession of the council's land, which he believed 'had been done this week'. The contractor had started work and some materials had arrived, he said, adding that sixteen-twentieths of the land had been acquired and paid for. His prediction that the railway would be completed by

25 March 1902, probably a contractual obligation, turned out to be mistaken.

Earlier, on 1 March 1901, Charles David Szlumper, Sir James's eldest son and the resident engineer, had written to Thomas E. Owen seeking 'a couple of smart men' able to speak English for survey work to start on 4 March, so presumably construction activity had followed the surveyors. In 1911 Owen gave his occupation as 'county road surveyor' so he was probably working on his own account ten years earlier.

Work had definitely started by 28 March, when the *Welsh Gazette* reported that Pethick Brothers were at work on both the Devil's Bridge and harbour lines. By working from each end and in each direction from the centre, it said, four gangs would be working simultaneously, hastening the work.

Advertisements in the *Cambrian News* on 12 April indicated progress too. One sought two reliable permanent way men, while the other sought 10,000 fir sleepers, 4ft 6in x 9in x 4½in.

Despite the assumed support of their nominees, it was not long before the contractors were in dispute with the company. By 26 April 1901 £3,600 due under the terms of the 21 December agreement had not been paid and a report on progress obtained by Szlumper varied greatly from one submitted by the resident engineer, his son. After the threat of legal action, the money was paid by the end of June and on 11 July was allocated to the share accounts of the brothers equally, a transaction which demonstrates how the contractors underwrote the shares. It was a money-go-round. Pethick Brothers would buy the shares, presumably with borrowed money, and the company would pay Pethick Brothers.

Another matter dealt with on 26 April was a letter from the Midland Railway Carriage & Wagon Company of Shrewsbury, offering for sale 'some trucks on hand made for the Plynlimon & Hafan Railway Company'. £137 10s was paid for them on 24 September.

A matter not recorded as dealt with by the directors was the application for another light railway order on 1 May 1901. Chiefly it sought powers to substitute the bridges by level crossings, to extend the time for purchasing land for the Aberaeron extension, and to construct, work and maintain both the Devil's Bridge line and the Aberaeron extension as light railways, in accordance with the Light Railways Act.

The directors visited Aberystwyth for the first time on 29 May 1901, examining the works in progress. Smith and Madge were also guests at a banquet held to mark the start of the town's promenade extension. According to the *Welsh Gazette* published on 16 May they would have seen track running parallel to the Cambrian Railways, nearly to Llanbadarn. While there the directors agreed to form a finance and general purposes committee comprising Smith, Francis and Madge, any two to form a quorum. The committee was to deal with all matters relating to the railway's construction, equipment and payment therefore. It met for the first time on 19 June 1901.

On that occasion payment of £3,000 to Pethick Brothers was approved following presentation of Szlumper's first certificate and orders for 'trucks, carriages and engines' sanctioned. Some landowners and their tenants were not being as cooperative as they might have been, and it had been necessary to pay both parties to gain access. In one case land owned by Emily Jenkins was occupied by the Reverend Thomas Jenkyns; she was paid £400 and he received £350.

Notwithstanding the earlier agreement with the Board of Trade concerning the harbour branch route around 'the gap', when Pethick Brothers reached that spot in April, 'certain persons' claiming mooring rights stopped further progress. Despatching an inspector to assess the situation, in May the Board of Trade reported that it understood that if the railway was laid out just below the high-water mark the company would lower an area on the east of the harbour and improve the area around the entrance to the gap in compensation. It was also expected to make a crossing over the rails to preserve the existing right of way. The council referred the matter to a committee and nothing more was said about it.

The Manchester & Milford Railway bridge was erected on 23 June. The *Welsh Gazette*, 27 June 1901, said that the work had to be carried out between the last train on Saturday night and the first on Monday morning and that despite inclement weather it was completed by 7pm on the Sunday. The paper also said that the bridge was the most expensive item on the railway.

On 4 July, the paper also reported that three locomotives had been ordered from the local firm of Williams & Metcalfe, although they would be constructed at the Patent Steam Exhaust Injector Company's works in Manchester. The paper had got the company name wrong, it was actually the Patent Exhaust Steam Injector Company; founded in 1878, it was renamed Davies & Metcalfe in 1902, the Davies element in recognition of the support given by the contractor David Davies and his son Edward.

James Metcalfe, the company's founder, had been born in Oswestry in 1847. Moving to Aberystwyth as the Manchester & Milford Railway's locomotive foreman in 1869, he invented an exhaust steam injector to deliver water to steam locomotive boilers, obtaining patents in 1875-7 which were sold to the Patent company in 1878. Williams & Metcalfe was the engineering business located at the Rheidol Foundry formed by Metcalfe when he left the MMR in 1882.

John Jones, a stone mason working on the Rheidol river bridge, performed an act of heroism on 8 July 1901, reported the *Welsh Gazette* (11 July). Seeing one of the boys playing in the river getting into difficulty he jumped in and rescued him from the bottom of a pool. Trained in artificial resuscitation by the St John's Ambulance Association, Jones prepared to act but the child revived on his own and was sent home.

On the same date, Szlumper told the directors about an inspection that he had made the previous week, explaining that although a 'fair amount of work had been done' he regretted that at the current rate of progress, and bearing in mind that the working days would be getting shorter, it would be impossible for the line to be completed by the specified date, March 1902. Certificate No 2 (£2,400) was paid at the same time. On 12 July the *Cambrian News* reported that the line extended for two miles from Aberystwyth and that about 1½ miles had been built between Abernant and Aberffrwd.

Submitting certificate No 3 (£1,200) on 14 August, the Szlumpers reported that little work had been carried out since the last meeting. In their opinion this was because the contractors did not have enough men on the contract. John Pethick, who was present, said that they had tried to employ more men and were paying higher rates than normal in the locality, but the situation would not improve until the harvest was completed; an advertisement for labour placed in the *Cambrian News* on 12 July had attracted several striking quarrymen from the Penrhyn slate quarry but not enough to progress the railway at the desired rate. Writing in 1943, in a brief history of the railway composed for W.E. Heyward, creator of the WEH-Lyn Collection now housed at the National Archives, James Rees, the railway's first manager, said that the labour situation improved after men no longer needed on the Elan valley reservoir contracts were taken on. They were rough men, he said, and no-one wanted them as lodgers, so they lived in huts obtained from the Elan valley contractors.

Pethick insisted that they would meet the contract deadline of having the line ready for inspection by 31 March 1902, a position he repeated on 30 October in the face of the engineers' continued doubts. Certificate No 4, for £1,200, had been submitted on 3 October.

In August J.B. Sunders had been given the order, valued at £1,167 8s 4d, to supply and install the railway's signalling, and Midland Railway Carriage & Wagon was to supply two timber trucks (£59 each) and three passenger brake vans (£79 each).

The arrival of a locomotive to assist Pethick Brothers' efforts was reported by the *Welsh Gazette* on 5 September 1901. A Bagnall 2-4-0T built in 1897, it already had a varied history and was on its third gauge and third name. Built in 750mm (2ft 5½in) gauge for a Brazilian sugar plantation, and named *Treze de Maio*, the order was cancelled before it could be despatched. Soon afterwards it was regauged to 2ft 3in and sold to the Plynlimon & Hafan Railway, a short-lived railway intended to serve the nearby, ten miles north of Devil's Bridge, and equally short-lived Hafan granite quarry, where it was named *Talybont*. Returned to its maker in 1899, it was re-gauged again and named *Rheidol* for Pethick Brothers.

Reports concerning the navvies appeared in the newspapers between September 1901 and May 1902, usually concerning drink or its aftermath.

The most important incident, headlined 'the shebeening case' when it arrived at court in November 1901, concerned William Cann, Pethick Brothers' foreman ganger, who was accused of selling intoxicating liquor, beer, without a licence at Gamlyn House, near Aberffrwd, where he lived with his wife.

Bagnall 2-4-0T *Talybont*, which became the Vale of Rheidol Railway's No 3 *Rheidol*, at Bwlch Glas on the Plynlimon & Hafan Railway on 19 August 1897. This 2ft 3in gauge, 8¾ miles-long railway had the shortest existence imaginable. A passenger service was started on 28 March 1898 and ended on 6 August the same year. Goods traffic probably followed the delivery of the first steam locomotive in 1897 and was ended in the summer of 1899. Pethick Brothers bought the locomotive, Bagnall 2-4-0T *Talybont* after it had been regauged and renamed it *Rheidol*.

A view down the Rheidol valley from above Aberffrwd in 1903. The location of Gamlyn House, the site of the 'shebeen', is indicated. (Henry Hicks Davies)

An extract from the Ordnance Survey 1904 6in map showing the locations of Dol Gamlyn and Gamlyn House, identified as Gamlyn Cottage by the OS, in relation to Aberffrwd station. (Ordnance Survey)

Gamlyn House

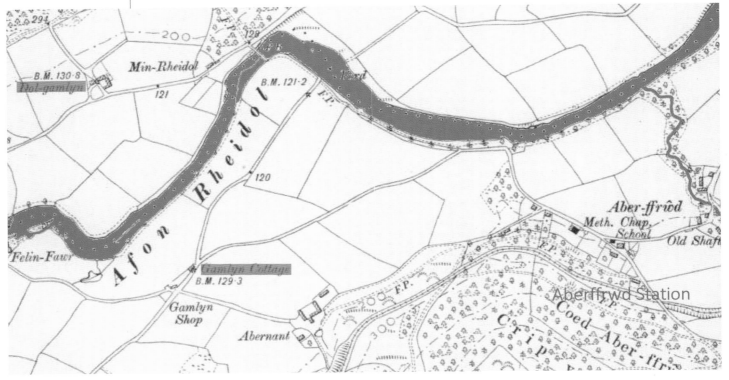

A police officer gave evidence that he had kept watch on the house, had heard beer being ordered and seen it being paid for. Two weeks later three officers had watched the house, raiding it when they saw beer being brought out, finding four nine-gallon casks, two full, one half-full and one empty, which they confiscated.

Providing an insight into priorities, the prosecuting solicitor pointed out that it was a serious case, complaining that it was hard enough for the police to keep watch on licensed premises without having to go to – remote was implied – Cwmrheidol to watch unlicensed ones.

For Cann, it was explained that he had worked for Pethick Brothers for twelve years and had been asked to live in the valley. Renting Gamlyn, he opened a convenience store for the navvies, and because they found it difficult to obtain lodgings, provided accommodation for six of them. He had refused to supply his lodgers with beer, but they had clubbed together to buy it, and he or his wife fetched it from Aberystwyth with other supplies. The arrangement was no different, argued his solicitor, than that which existed at working men's clubs. However, the magistrates found the case proved and fined Cann £5.

His appeal was allowed at the Cardigan Quarter Sessions at Lampeter in January 1902 though, the chairman saying that if he had heard the case in the first instance, he thought that he would not have convicted. But Cann had to pay his own costs. An account about the railway published in the *Aberystwyth Observer* on 29 May 1902 said that Pethick Brothers had not been able to get men to work on the deep cutting near Aberffrwd because there was no public house nearby, and that that was the reason the 'club' was established.

Other cases were more straightforward. In September 1901, John Dyer was involved in an altercation with a farmer over the provision of transport, bound over to keep the peace for five years, and Jesse Teuton and David Jones were both fined 1s, the first for begging, the second for being drunk and

incapable on the highway. Only Jones was linked to the railway in the *Welsh Gazette's* report but as Teuton was from Plymouth it was the most likely reason for him being in the area. The town council had also complained about the number of vagrants in the area, attracted by the railway.

James Brown and Thomas Johnson had left the district when they were fined 5s each, and costs, in their absence at Llanbadarn magistrates' court on 28 November 1901. A policeman said that he had found them lying in the road about a mile from Devil's Bridge, where they had been working on the railway.

In January 1902 members of the public helped the police to carry navvies John Murphy, Joseph Bulger and John Baron to the police station when they became violent after being evicted from the Lion Vaults in Aberystwyth. They were fined 5s or 10s for being drunk and disorderly plus £1 plus costs for assaulting the police, or 14 days or one month hard labour respectively in default. Ann Murphy, Murphy's wife, charged with being drunk and disorderly and obstructing the police, was bound over.

In November 1901, it was the landlord of the Goginan Arms Hotel, Ponterwyd, who found himself in court, charged with selling beer during prohibited hours on a Sunday. When the police admitted that they had seen neither beer being dispensed nor money changing hands the case was dismissed. Four of the customers had been navvies; the landlord had called for assistance because he thought he might have difficulty persuading them to leave.

A *Welsh Gazette* report on 12 December 1901 concerned Sunday drinking, which it said had become prevalent in the Rheidol valley since railway construction had started. Two labourers had been arrested in Pontrhydygroes charged with being drunk and disorderly, a third with being drunk. John Murphy, again, received 28 days with hard labour, he had scuffled with the police when arrested, and Robert Williams and Robert Lloyd received 14 days each. The magistrates wanted an investigation into the source of the drink; publicans were allowed to serve *bona fide* travellers but not to make men drunk, they declared.

The last case concerned Robert Williams, again, and William Williams who had refused to disperse when found quarrelling and creating a disturbance in Mill Street, Aberystwyth, on 27 April 1902, another Sunday. Both were jailed, 28 days and 14 days respectively, when they were unable to pay the fines levied.

Considering the number of men employed on the railway, as many as 350 were reported, drink was probably not a big problem; only a few cases reached the courts, but it was a contributory factor in the deaths of three men, despite the evidence in one case.

Thomas Jackson had been found dead in the river near Capel Bangor on 17 September 1901. Hearing evidence that he had been sober when he had left the pub the previous evening, the inquest jury returned a verdict 'found drowned'; he had probably fallen from the footbridge crossing the river in the dark.

Samuel Wilson had died on 7 December 1901 when he fell from a cart that its driver had invited him to ride on when he had asked for directions to Devil's Bridge. The driver gave evidence that Wilson had been drinking before he met him and after he climbed onto the cart. Aged 35, Wilson had been working on the railway for less than a week and had revealed very little about himself to his new colleagues.

Thought to have been from Lincolnshire, Frank Watts had been working on the railway for two months when he died. He had been paid at 2.30pm on 4 January 1902, Saturday, and had been drinking. Walking through an incomplete cutting near Devil's Bridge instead of taking the path to his lodgings at Troedrhiwfron, he lost his balance and fell into the ravine, falling about 300ft. Never regaining consciousness, despite the surgeon at Aberystwyth infirmary trepanning his skull, he died at 6.30am the next day, aged 52. He is buried in an unmarked grave at Aberystwyth's public cemetery.

Another aspect of the navvies' lives was highlighted by a report on a meeting of the Aberystwyth Urban District Council under the heading 'unsanitary dwellings' (*Welsh Gazette* 31 October 1901). The inspector of nuisances had been called to Dol Gamlyn in Cwmrheidol, close to Gamlyn House, the 'shebeen', when he found a three-bedroom dwelling occupied by eighteen persons. The tenant was employed on the railway; he lived there with his wife and eight children and eight lodgers. One of the councillors said that there were other properties equally bad and that the report was the result of jealousy and malice against strangers. The inspector was directed to serve a notice restricting the number of occupants.

The navvies apparently caused no trouble at the Hafod Arms Hotel, for on 26 December 1901 sixty of them were treated to dinner by the landlord and his wife. There was probably a sigh of relief when they left though. At the Devil's Bridge eisteddfod in October 1902 a prize was awarded for the best epitaph to the navvy. Other prizes were awarded for the best four verses in Welsh on 'The advent of the train to Devil's Bridge' and a dialogue on the advantages or disadvantages of the Rheidol Light Railway to Devil's Bridge.

After heavy rain the Rheidol valley was susceptible to flooding, the *Cambrian News* reporting two instances a week apart in November 1901. Both reports mentioned that the railway formation had been affected but had stood up well to the inundation.

By 12 December 1901, when the directors met, Pethick Brothers' share accounts were in arrears to the extent of £22,860. Certificate No 5 (£1,500) had been submitted a month earlier and paid, and was followed by No 6 (£1,240) in December. Having bought 'plant and material' for the railway the contractors asked for an extra certificate to be issued, in order that they could be reimbursed. The request was passed to the directors who approved a certificate being issued for £7,000. The contractors also asked for more trucks, an order being placed with Midland Railway Carriage & Wagon for five to be delivered before the end of the year.

Looking to the future, the directors resolved to appoint a traffic superintendent, choosing

Railway News, the *People* (once each) and the *Western Mail* (twice) in which to advertise. All applicants were to be Welsh speakers, the successful candidate being offered a salary of £200. An advertisement also appeared in the *Evening Express* on 16 December.

On 18 February 1902 the appointment of James Rees was approved subject to a satisfactory medical certificate being submitted and a fidelity guarantee of £250 being obtained. The appointment would take effect from 1 May 1902, the first admission that Pethick Brothers would be unable to complete their work by 31 March.

In choosing Rees, the directors thought that it was important for the post holder to have a good knowledge of the area and the traders, and those who might use the railway. Born in 1872, the son of a Lampeter nurseryman, he had worked for the Manchester & Milford Railway for 13 years, moving to Aberystwyth and becoming its *de facto* deputy manager. The *Evening Express* claimed that there had been 54 applications for the post, while the *Welsh Gazette* said that only two of them had been interviewed. While waiting to take up his appointment Rees was expected to report on staff requirements, wages to be paid, train working '&c &c'.

Still on 18 February, Pethick Brothers were paid £9,000 against certificate No 9 without comment. On 30 January the *Aberystwyth Observer* had reported that rails had reached Capel Bangor, five miles from Aberystwyth, and anticipated a locomotive reaching Devil's Bridge in March, 'unless the weather is very bad'. Given that it was winter it seems hard to believe that they had achieved this amount of work since December. One certificate appears to have been missed or mis-numbered. The SS *Abbotsford* had delivered 250 tons of rail on 16 February.

Two men were injured in the spring of 1902. Albert Went, a carpenter, was treated at the infirmary for a gash to his lower jaw caused by a circular saw at Devil's Bridge in March, and William Evans was caught by a blast in a cutting in April. With wounds to his head, left eye, face and hands, as well as losing several teeth, he was also treated at the infirmary.

James Rees, the railway's manager throughout its independent existence, aged 48.

Another navvy was in the news for a different reason, also in April. Timothy Richards made the mistake of returning to his home territory when he deserted from the navy, working on the railway since January. Unfortunately for him, he was recognised by a policeman who knew that he had joined the navy. When he failed to produce his discharge papers, he was arrested to be court-martialled.

H.H.M. Smith, the chairman, had spent five days in Aberystwyth over Easter, 27-31 March 1902, telling his colleagues on 26 April that he had gone over the works with J.W. Szlumper and that 'progress was not as satisfactory as desired'. Pethick Brothers were to be told to do whatever was required to have the line ready for inspection by 22 May. This had little effect and on 14 May the engineers told the directors that without another engine the line would not be ready for the summer. The contractors had not been able to find another loco and had sought to make an agreement with Davies & Metcalfe to use one of the company's locos. The directors agreed to this providing Pethick Brothers gave an undertaking that the line would be ready by 1 July. Szlumper's certificate No 10, £2,000, was approved and paid.

Funding arrangements for the locomotives were put in place on 26 April 1902. Davies & Metcalfe Limited had agreed to accept part payment in the form of two £500 Lloyds 4% bonds payable on 15 July 1903. The company built no other locomotives and the only other known locomotive work carried out was the overhaul of the North Wales Narrow Gauge Railways single Fairlies in 1902 and 1903.

Ellis and Cottier proposed that the company borrow £1,000 on the directors' personal guarantees, the money to be paid to Davies & Metcalfe in exchange for the Lloyd bonds, these to be held by the directors until they had been repaid. By 9 June 1902, a £5,000 overdraft had been arranged with the National Provincial Bank for a period of 12 months.

There were signs that the railway would soon be ready for opening. Acetylene was ordered for lighting, a water supply was arranged at Devil's Bridge, a local contractor erected a carriage shed at Capel Bangor, leaving the question of who would pay for it in abeyance, and Pethick Brothers excavated a weighbridge pit, paid for as an extra. R. Roberts & Sons was paid £31 2s 6d for the shed and Henry Pooley & Son £56 for the weighbridge.

'The roadway has been roughly made all the way to the Devil's Bridge, and rails have been laid beyond Aberffrwd,' reported the *Aberystwyth Observer* on 8 May. It also expected a locomotive to traverse the entire line by the end of the month and for the railway to be finished by 'Coronation day', 26 June. Due to the King's illness the coronation was postponed until 9 August at short notice, but the railway was not complete for that date either. The first loco, *Edward VII*, was delivered on 30 May, reported the *Welsh Gazette* on 5 June 1902, adding that 'a good deal of the rolling stock has already been delivered', but not as much as that sweeping statement might imply, as it was not until 26 June that the same paper was able to say that three, of twelve, passenger carriages had arrived.

A Plynlimon & Hafan Railway wagon come to grief on the outskirts of Aberystwyth during the railway's construction. The locomotive is *Edward VII*. (Vale of Rheidol Railway collection)

Edward VII, the first of the railway's Davies & Metcalfe locomotives. As 2-6-2Ts, they bore visual similarities to the Lynton & Barnstaple Railway's Manning, Wardle locomotives, and it is probably not irrelevant that J.W. Szlumper was the engineer of both railways. (John Scott Morgan collection)

Prince of Wales, the second 2-6-2T, at Davies & Metcalfe's Romiley, Manchester, works. The nameplate looks as though it was changed before the loco was delivered.

An account of a trip on a works train from Aberystwyth to Aberffrwd was published in the *Aberystwyth Observer* on 29 May. Saying that he had been given permission by Pethick Brothers to travel whenever he liked, the writer described going to the station on 'Saturday afternoon', 24 May was most likely, where he was joined by Rees. Travelling in an open wagon in preference to riding on the locomotive's footplate, he noted 'a couple of trucks laden with rails' behind him. The train went as far as Aberffrwd, where he and Rees walked along the formation for about a mile.

Reviewing the situation on 9 June 1902, the directors formed the opinion that the engineers had not taken such steps as the contract permitted to ensure that the railway had been completed by 31 March and that the interests of the shareholders were suffering as a result.

On 25 June the engineers reported that they had inspected the line and thought that it would be completed by 12 July. On hearing that Davies & Metcalfe had written to say that the second loco, *Prince of Wales*, would be ready about 16 July, the directors asked for overtime to be worked to complete it sooner.

Expenditure to June 1902 exceeded the available capital of £44,140 by around £2,000, a position that was eased by the £5,000 overdraft and which would be improved further when the £6,860 arrears in calls for the shares were paid. No doubt the contractors were responsible for most, if not all, of the arrears. Attention was turned to the company's £17,000 unissued 4% debentures, Cottier saying that his firm (Lane & Cottier, stockbrokers?) had clients who might be interested in buying the issue if terms could be arranged. His co-directors agreed to accept not less than £90 per £100. Cottier, however, was mistaken about his firm's clients' interest in the debentures for by 21 October it had withdrawn from attempting to place them.

Tranship facilities in the harbour were dealt with by the council's harbour committee at the end of June 1902,

responding to a letter from Rees earlier in the month. It appears that the railway extended to a point beyond the existing wharf where the water depth was inadequate; he wanted the wharf to be improved to accommodate ships of at least 400 tons. The borough surveyor was instructed to produce plans but the councillors were reluctant to commit the estimated £1,000 expenditure without receiving any commitment for a minimum tonnage.

The second light railway order was made on 1 August 1902, apparently only after an Irish MP had asked a question about the length of time it was taking to make it in the House of Commons on 10 July. An inquiry had been held in Aberystwyth on 21 October and the light railway commissioners had submitted it to the Board of Trade for confirmation on 21 March. After the usual period for objections the Board had decided to seek further information about the scheme's financial viability. The order was then placed in abeyance until the Devil's Bridge line had been inspected.

At the inquiry, A.J. Hughes, the solicitor, had recited the company's case, adding that the extension was unlikely to be built without a Treasury grant. Examined about the level crossings, W.W. Szlumper had offered to leave two of the bridges on the Aberaeron line.

There were no objections there but on 14 May 1902 the promoters of a standard gauge line from Aberystwyth to New Quay submitted a petition against the order to the Board of Trade, claiming, *inter alia*, that the company would never be able to raise the required capital, that a narrow gauge line would not adequately benefit the locality, and that their standard gauge proposal would be better. Although they were ruled out of time the company was instructed to respond to the petition and to give proof of its financial ability to carry out its undertakings.

The company's hopes of obtaining funding from other sources were soon dashed. The Treasury ruled that it was not an 'existing railway company' as defined

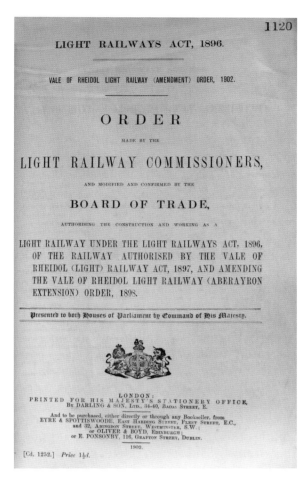

The 1902 light railway order.

by the Light Railways Act and the county council disputed the company's claim that it had agreed to make an advance, saying that it had merely agreed to the company obtaining the power for it to do so.

The point about the 'existing railway company' was to do with the company's desire to obtain a 'special advance' as permitted by clause No 5 of the Light Railways Act. This enabled the Boards of Agriculture or Trade to certify that a proposed light railway would benefit agriculture, the first, be a necessary means of communication between a fishing harbour or village and a market or necessary for the development or maintenance of some industry, the second, to qualify it for a free grant from the Treasury.

There were several provisos, one being that the proposed railway must be constructed and worked by 'a railway company existing'. As the Light Railways Act did not contain a definition for an existing railway company the decision on this point seems to have been improper.

Another proviso was that the land must be provided free of charge. To undermine the company's position in this regard, a solicitor wrote, after the inquiry, that his client and other landowners intended to claim full compensation and damages for severance. Losing the Clause No 5 free grant, the company said that it would apply for a loan under the terms of Clause No 4.

Despite the uncertainty about funding, Major Edward Druitt was sent to make a preliminary inspection of the Devil's Bridge line, making it on 18 July, six days after the engineers had told the directors the line would be finished. He found that the formation had been completed throughout, with rails laid up to 10 miles 33 chains. Track laying had just been started from Devil's Bridge. Ballasting had been completed for 5½ miles and partially carried out for a further five miles; the track still needed lifting in places though. He had been told that the second-hand flat-bottom rails weighed between 52 and 56 lbs per yard. The sleepers were 4ft 6in x 9in x 4½in uncreosoted Baltic fir or larch laid at 3ft 6in centres. The rails were spiked to the sleepers with iron spikes and base plates. 4in coach screws were used at the joints. There were too few sleepers in some locations. Drainage, especially in cuttings, was insufficient but would be attended to with the ballasting. Fencing was nearly done. Including the termini, there were five stations.

The line was to be worked with Tyer's electric tablet system, Capel Bangor being the passing place. Aberystwyth, Capel Bangor and Devil's Bridge were provided with signals and ground frames; at the other places the point levers were controlled by the section tablet. All the stations were lit by acetylene gas and had shelters. Telephone communication was to be provided between the stations and the telephone poles had been erected for 9½ miles with the wires run out for five miles.

There was one underbridge, across the Rheidol. It had eight timber trestles and timber longitudinals. There was one overbridge where the line was crossed by the Manchester & Milford Railway; he had not overlooked the overbridge at Devil's Bridge, that was installed later. There were a few culverts. Some of the cuttings needed trimming to give adequate clearances for the carriages. The level crossings had cattle guards instead of gates. He thought that they were safe, the roads being little used, and saw no need for gates.

The locomotives and carriages had been delivered and were equipped with vacuum brakes. The carriages had centre buffer couplings and 'They appear very suitable for the line.'

The railway, he summarised, appeared to be well constructed as far as it was finished, but a good deal of work was still required in platelaying, ballasting and drainage, before it could be approved for passenger traffic.

The new order permitted three more years to complete the extension land purchases and four more years for its construction. The county council was authorised to advance up to £18,000 for the extension and to borrow money for the purpose. The 1897 railway was allowed to be constructed and worked as a light railway, with its bridges replaced by open level crossings. Notwithstanding its legal status as a light railway, the railway had always been promoted as simply 'the Vale of Rheidol Railway'.

C.C. Green (see Bibliography), incidentally, claimed that the railway had been subject to deception and that some of the rail weighed as little as 32lbs per yard. With a locomotive axle loading of 4.4 tons, higher maintenance costs might have been expected if this was the case; it was 1906 before any new rail was bought. The North Wales Narrow Gauge Railways, not known for spending money unnecessarily, required 41lb rail for an axle loading of 2.8 tons. Druitt could also be expected to tell the difference between rail weighing over 50lbs and rail as light as 32lbs on sight. Green also referred to an account

of this inspection that states that several derailments occurred in Druitt's presence. As the ballasting was incomplete this probably should not be too much of a surprise.

No doubt the contractors and the workforce celebrated on 28 July when the track laying was completed. The *Aberystwyth Observer* (31 July 1902) reported that 'the engines are running up there [to Devil's Bridge] daily', adding that ballasting was expected to be completed in a fortnight and that passenger trains might be running by 15 August, or sooner. Describing the locomotives' use of side tanks to enable them to run without taking water intermediately, the paper observed, 'To this extent beauty has been somewhat sacrificed to utility.' They were, it said, painted in khaki, relieved by chocolate and olive green.

On 5 August J.W. and W.W. Szlumper informed the directors that the works were complete except for some ballasting, which they expected to be completed by 12 August, the day fixed for the inspection. They added that, 'both engines and all the rolling stock … have been delivered upon the ground.' The return of working stock made at the end of the year declared two locomotives, 12 carriages, 15 wagons, three passenger brake vans and three timber trucks. The company notified the Board of Trade that it expected to commence public operations from 10 September.

Druitt visited twice more. Unfortunately the Board of Trade file concerning the railway's construction and inspections is missing or miscatalogued. The preliminary inspection report is in the amendment order file but, fortunately, a separate file of transcripts of inspection reports contains Druitt's reports dated 14 August and 25 November 1902.

On the first occasion, 12 August, he was accompanied by Smith and one of the other directors and by the engineers and contractors. Although he did not comment on it, there was naturally little progress compared with his July visit. Railway No 2, the harbour branch, was not inspected as it was not to be used by passengers. The junction between the two was worked by a single-lever groundframe unlocked by the Aberystwyth-Capel Bangor tablet.

The railway was 11 miles 59½ chains long and rose 669ft, he reported. The sharpest curve was 3 chains radius and the steepest gradient 1 in 50, in one place for a distance of nearly four miles with some sharp reverse curves. The last seven miles was cut into the valley side, in some places precipitous. The highest embankment was 68ft and the deepest cutting 39ft. The Rheidol river bridge had seven 16ft spans. Both it and the Manchester & Milford Railway's overbridge had sufficient theoretical strength.

The passing loop at Capel Bangor was worked by a nine-lever ground frame with two spare levers. The down home signal required moving so that it could be seen for 440 yards. The siding at Nantyronen was also worked by a single lever locked by the tablet. Devil's Bridge had sidings worked from a five-lever ground frame and a crossover for the loco run-round worked by hand.

The first five miles of track was in good order, but the remainder was unfinished,

sleepers insufficiently packed and rails not set to line. Broken stone ballast needed breaking up and some sleepers were 'much below specified width' and in some places too far apart. On curves of less than five chains radius the sleepers should be not more than 3ft apart. On all curves on high banks and 'where the side of the valley is precipitous' check rails were required.

Clearances in the cuttings were still inadequate. The trap points in the engine shed siding and at Nantyronen needed to be double bladed and made to run off at a sharper angle or moved further from the junction. Carriage running boards fouled the running line when stabled in the loop at Aberystwyth; it needed to be slewed. Druitt was particularly unhappy about the way the culvert at Llanbadarn had been bridged, it was a poor piece of workmanship and should be altered, he said.

The railway was unfinished, he concluded, and it would be unsafe for the public to use it. The company withdrew its statutory notice of intent to open to passengers.

Prince of Wales and a short train on the approach to Devil's Bridge. The stationary train and the posed personnel are indicative of the photograph being taken before the railway was opened. (Vale of Rheidol Railway collection)

Although the railway was not approved for the carriage of passengers, there was a consequence of the inspection. The *Aberystwyth Observer*, 14 August, announced, 'This line is now opened for goods traffic,' while the *Welsh Gazette*, on the same date, said, 'The company … are now in the position to deal with goods traffic.' Two weeks later, the former said that the goods traffic was exceeding expectations and speculated that more wagons would be needed.

Under the headline 'To Devil's Bridge by rail. By one who has been there,' an *Aberystwyth Observer* correspondent described the journey he had made on 13 September. 'All the heavy work has been completed,' he wrote, 'and gangs of men are giving the finishing touches to the road.' He had no idea when passenger services would start but said that the company wished to use it as much as possible with goods traffic to be sure that everything was in good order. He also

commented on the newly constructed road bridge at Devil's Bridge, saying that it was a great improvement and its height above its predecessor improved the view. On 27 September, A.J. Hughes, the town clerk and the company's local solicitor, and a group of friends also experienced the rail journey to Devil's Bridge.

Meeting on 21 October, the directors instructed the engineers to give the

Although the railway's crest proudly proclaims that the company was incorporated in 1897, it was obviously not created until after 1901, when the third bridge was built.

The company's seal was based on the same design. (National Archives)

The Devil's Bridge soon after Cardiganshire County Council had built its new bridge in 1901. (Photochrom)

contractors a list of outstanding work and to enforce the contract. Had there really been nothing done since Druitt's visit in August? Certificate No 12 was approved and a cheque for £2,500 issued. Additional work sanctioned included ordering a bridge to cross the line at Devil's Bridge from Dorman, Long & Company, estimated cost, including installation, £70. A long list of payments approved included more signs of the impending opening: six station clocks, £16 10s; cylinder oil, £11 0s 11d; grease, £4 2s 1d; typewriting machine, £13 0s 0d; uniforms, £11 16s 6d.

An inaugural trip on 5 November was described in the *Welsh Gazette* the next day. Members of the town and county councils, land owners and others joined Smith, Charles Szlumper, 'Mr [John] Pethick' and Frank Pethick, who had managed the contract, for the journey. Refreshments were served at Devil's

Bridge and photographs were taken there. 'In all probability the line will be opened sometime this month.' The *Manchester Guardian* (7 November) said that in addition to capturing the 'enormous' summer passenger traffic to Devil's Bridge, the railway was expected to serve 'the more useful purpose of expediting the transit of lead ore from the mines, all of which are within a radius of four miles of the terminus.'

The *Cambrian News* (also 7 November) added that the train was hauled by *Edward VII* 'in charge of' James Metcalfe, whose company had built it; the guards had been Messrs Davies and Howe. The Aberystwyth station master was Thomas Gwyn Richards, formerly holding the same position at Glogue, Pembrokeshire, on the GWR, and the others were William Parkins, previously with the Festiniog Railway, and Arthur Evan Humphreys,

Dignitaries and others at Devil's Bridge on 5 November 1902. Of those seated on the second row, J.W. Szlumper is first left and John Pethick fourth left. Next to Szlumper is probably H.H.M. Smith, the chairman, in the centre C.D. Szlumper, the resident engineer, and on Pethick's left, his son N.F. Pethick, Pethick Brothers' 'man on the ground'. (Vale of Rheidol Railway collection)

The ladies in the party were photographed separately. It might be reasonable to suggest that those seated on chairs are J.W. Szlumpers' and John Pethick's wives.

formerly with the Cambrian Railways, at Capel Bangor and Devil's Bridge respectively. Already, it claimed, more lime had been conveyed to properties adjoining the railway than had been the case for many years, and coal was being sold at Devil's Bridge cheaper than it was in Aberystwyth. According to Green (see Bibliography), a second train was run for employees and families. The *Aberystwyth Observer* (13 November) added that the driver was Tom Savage, with Evan Lloyd Jones and Robert Davies as firemen.

Richards left the railway after three years, to work in the Manchester & Milford Railway's general manager's office, and died in 1909, aged 45. Parkins returned to the FR by September 1906. Humphreys took over as station master at Aberystwyth and returned to the Cambrian as station master at Dyffryn in 1917; he died in Borth in 1962.

Born in Llandinam in 1871, Thomas Hamer Savage, the driver, was a fitter at Metcalfe's Rheidol Foundry, where normally he would have been maintaining Manchester & Milford Railway locos. He did well for himself, moving into motor maintenance with his son; when he died in 1954 he lived at Sandmarsh Cottage, Queen's Road, Aberystwyth, which had been J.W. Szlumper's Aberystwyth home.

Meanwhile, the Cambrian Railways' directors were dealing with a request from Rees to provide and pay for an exchange siding at Plascrug. Writing on 11 November 1902, the Cambrian's general manager, Charles Sherwood Denniss, explained to his directors that Rees had said that the Cambrian should pay all the costs if it wanted Rheidol traffic as it could already exchange traffic with the Manchester & Milford Railway. A siding would cost £150; he did not recommend it as the

In Loving Memory of
MARY
WIFE OF THOMAS HAMER SAVAGE
SAND MARSH, QUEEN'S RD ABERYSTWYTH.
DIED JUNE 22 1942
AGED 69 YEARS.
WORTHY OF REMEMBRANCE.
ALSO THE ABOVE
THOMAS HAMER SAVAGE
DIED MARCH 8. 1954,
AGED 86 YEARS.
REST IN PEACE.
ALSO THEIR LOVING SON
EDWARD OWEN SAVAGE
DIED APRIL 21. 1999,
AGED 92 YEARS.
DEVOTED HUSBAND OF NELL
AND DEARLY LOVED FATHER OF
MARY, HELEN AND JANET.

railway's future was uncertain – he gave no explanation for this assertion but his directors must have thought the investment worth making because he was instructed to agree terms in February 1903.

After some correspondence, Smith sent a sealed agreement which Denniss rejected for being 'arbitrary, one-sided and generally unsatisfactory'. Sufficient progress was made for the railway to carry out the work (*Welsh Gazette* 23 April 1903) at a cost of £47 10s for the turnout and groundframe, but faced with the Cambrian's refusal to use it without an agreement Smith wrote to Denniss on 28 November 1903 and threatened to have it removed. A contribution of £26 was made to the Cambrian's expenses and the Cambrian directors resolved to seal the agreement on 20 January 1904. Rees

appears to have overlooked informing the Board of Trade about the siding.

By the 11 November 1902 directors' meeting, Smith had dealt with 'numerous' complaints made by the contractors that the locomotives were damaging the track. To determine if they had any foundation, he had obtained a set of drawings and submitted them to Messrs Hawkshaw & Dobson for an opinion, Hawkshaw being president of the Institution of Civil Engineers. No obvious fault was found in the drawings, the rails were more than adequate, and as the locomotives' wheelbase was only 6ft, curves of three chain radius could be traversed. It might be worth while turning down the flanges on the centre wheelsets if it had not been done, he thought. 'It is possible that the permanent way may require fresh

Thomas Hamer Savage, who drove the first trains as an employee of James Metcalfe's Rheidol Foundry and who probably trained the railway's first drivers, is buried in Aberystwyth's public cemetery.

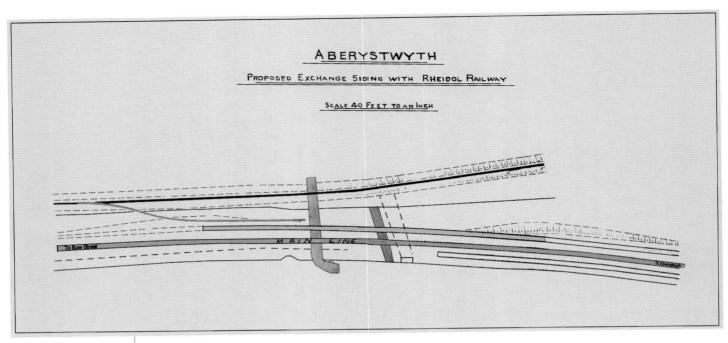

ABERYSTWYTH

PROPOSED EXCHANGE SIDING WITH RHEIDOL RAILWAY

SCALE 40 FEET TO AN INCH

The Cambrian Railways' plan of the exchange siding at Plascrug. (National Archives)

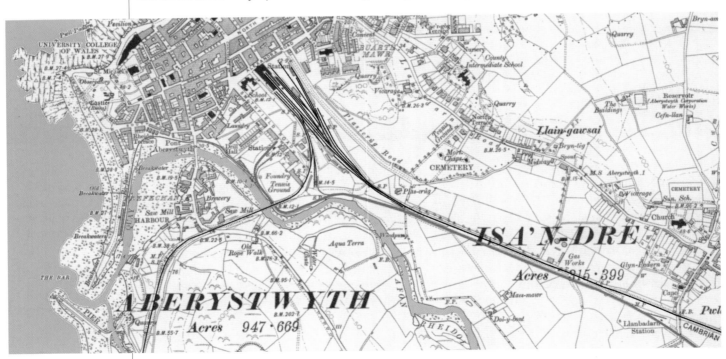

An extract from the Ordnance Survey's 6in sheet of Aberystwyth, 1904 revision, showing the railway between the harbour and Llanbadarn. (Ordnance Survey)

alignment as it is often found that the curves are distorted by slewing and are actually sharper than originally set out.'

There appeared to be some issue with the carriages. Smith reported a meeting with the Midland Railway Carriage & Wagon Company and the engineers were 'requested to report at an early date upon the carriages and whether they had been placed in a condition to enable them to work satisfactory [sic] …' Subsequently, Williams & Metcalfe's account for 'making the necessary repairs' to 'trucks', £81, was passed to the maker.

Considering a possible opening date, assuming the forthcoming inspection was satisfactory, the directors resolved to open immediately for goods and to defer opening for passengers until 1 January 1903. A report in the *Aberystwyth Observer* (27 November 1902) explained that the reason for wanting to defer the opening was to avoid having to set up accounts and make Board of Trade returns for just a few weeks.

Smith also reported that he had met the county council's finance committee concerning the £700 cost of re-surveying the Aberaeron extension. Subsequently the council had agreed to contribute £600 and he had provisionally committed the company to the remainder, making it clear to the council, he told his fellow directors,

that Devil's Bridge capital and revenue could not be used on the extension.

Druitt made his final inspection on 25 November, submitting his report on the same day. A good-sized party accompanied him: Smith, the chairman, Sir J.W. Szlumper and C.D. Szlumper, engineers, A.J. Hughes, the solicitor, 'Mr Pethick', the contractor, and Rees, the traffic superintendent. He tested the Rheidol river bridge, which he had not done previously, and was satisfied with the results, although one of the trestles showed signs of scour. Installation of the tablet instruments and telephones had been completed and his requirements of 14 August complied with except that four curves still required check rails. Imposing a speed limit of 10mph between Nantyronen and Devil's Bridge, except on the curves between 8¾ and 9 miles where he imposed 6mph, he recommended that approval be given to opening the line to passenger traffic.

A well-known photograph that epitomises the Vale of Rheidol Railway, taken before the railway was opened, although this version was not published until 1911. (James Valentine)

On the Way to Devil's Bridge, Aberystwyth

Szlumper's survey proved to be a masterful piece of work and should be ranked with the best narrow-gauge railway routes in the British Isles. From Aberystwyth the line ran through open countryside on easy gradients, reaching Capel Bangor (4½ miles) before it crossed a point 100ft above sea level. Reaching Nantyronen (6¾ miles, 200ft) required nearly half a mile of 1 in 40, and Aberffrwd (7¾ miles, 290ft) a short section of 1 in 48. From Aberffrwd, the railway ran along a ledge carved out of the hillside, a steady climb of 1 in 50 for just over four miles, before levelling out on the approach to Devil's Bridge (12 miles).

Signs that Pethick Brothers were winding down their operations were advertisements published in local newspapers: a stable for four horses, 28ft x 14ft, at Aberystwyth station yard (*Cambrian News* 14 November); a quantity of firewood at Aberystwyth station (*Welsh Gazette* 20 November); and an 8HP portable engine and saw bench at Devil's Bridge (*Cambrian News* 5 December).

Non-paying passengers were carried from Capel Bangor to Aberystwyth on 13 December. One hundred and twenty members of the 1st Cardigan Volunteer Artillery had marched from Aberystwyth and the train took them back, creating the railway's first link with the military.

Following representations from Rees, and subject to Druitt's requirements being met, Smith had agreed to the railway being opened to passengers from 22 December 1902, he told his colleagues on 5 December; presumably Rees could see benefit from the railway being able to carry passengers over the Christmas period. The engineers' certificate No 13, for £2,460, was approved and paid.

The directors were still keen to place the debentures; there were bills to be paid and the overdraft to be cleared. Once again Cottier said that his firm had clients who he thought would take them at 4% repayable in 1908, offering to try to place them provided the firm received a 10% brokerage fee and he was paid his incidental expenses. These terms being

RHEIDOL VALLEY & RAILWAY.

2-11155 J.V.

accepted, he agreed that if his clients wanted to go ahead, he would furnish their names and a £2,000 deposit by 8 December and the remainder by 12 December.

The cheque for £13,210 was handed over when the directors next met, on 16 December, Cottier having previously informed Smith that the investors were J.R. Pethick, N.F. Pethick, B.H. Pethick and John Pethick. So now the Pethick family owned the majority of the company's shares and all of its debt. Did the directors see it coming? The family, of course, was faced with the problem of getting the railway into a position where it was worth more than it had cost them to build it and could be sold for a profit.

The contractors then submitted a claim for extras amounting to £5,323 16s 9d, offering to withdraw it if they were relieved of their obligation to maintain the railway immediately and the final certificate, representing the retention, 10% of the contract, £4,500, issued. The directors pointed out that the contract provided for the maintenance and the retention and the request could not be accepted unless the company's interests were protected.

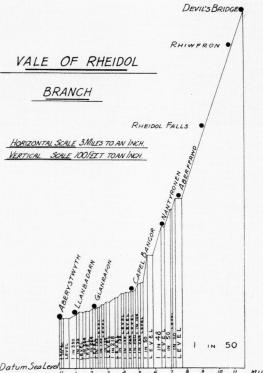

VALE OF RHEIDOL BRANCH

Horizontal Scale 3 Miles to an Inch.
Vertical Scale 100 Feet to an Inch.

This high-level view looking eastwards shows how skilfully Szlumper and Pethick Brothers carved a route out along the hillside. On the north side of the valley, the scars left by mining can be seen at two locations. The postcard was published in 1930. (James Valentine)

The railway's gradient profile. (National Archives)

Following 'considerable discussion' agreement was achieved: the certificate would be issued; when it had been paid the £1,900 due on Pethick Brothers' share

An unusual view of the Devil's Bridge locality looking south, taken soon after the railway was opened. The entrance to the station is on the left and the home and starting signals are visible. The bridge that crossed the railway, between the two signals, cost £70.

accounts would be paid; the company would be given a full receipt for all work carried out under the contract, including the extras; Pethick Brothers would be relieved from the maintenance liability forthwith; Pethick Brothers would transfer £2,000 of stock without charge as directed as a consideration for being released from the contract and three items still outstanding would be referred to J.W. Szlumper for arbitration, his decision to be final.

CHAPTER 3

THE INDEPENDENT YEARS

The first passenger train left Devil's Bridge at 8.30am on 22 December, carrying 17 passengers, reported the *Cambrian News* on 26 December, and reached Aberystwyth at 9.35am. The first departure from Aberystwyth was at 10.00, with 11 passengers including Smith and Rees.

Initially (*Welsh Gazette* 25 December) the timetable comprised three trains each way per day, 8.30am, 11.45am and 4.45pm from Devil's Bridge, and 10.00am, 2.15pm and 6.00pm from Aberystwyth. Green (See Bibliography) interpreted this as meaning that there were empty stock workings at the start and the end of the day, but it seems unlikely that an experienced railway operator like Rees, with his background of running the impecunious Manchester & Milford Railway, would have scheduled such unremunerative moves.

Two trains were also run on Christmas Day, attracting 150 passengers from Aberystwyth alone, reported the *Cambrian News* on 2 January 1902. Even more travelled the next day, requiring trains to be made up to five carriages, and on 8 January 1903 the *Aberystwyth Observer* said that the five-carriage train had run full.

The first Sunday train, an Aberystwyth-based working, had run on 28 December, attracting a 'crowd of people' who travelled, and a resolution in protest from the Tanycae Sunday School which was adopted by most Sunday schools and non-conformist

Edward VII with a long train, six carriages and two brake vans, at Aberystwyth early in 1903. At the end of March the office building, seen beyond the end of the train, was moved to the other side of the station's entrance. (John Scott Morgan collection)

A portrait of *Prince of Wales* in its original livery. The top of its tanks appears to be stacked with bags of kindling.

churches in the area. The paper thought that the objection was based on a fear that the trains would facilitate an increase in drunkenness. A 'railway official', Rees surely, asked, 'Why object to us more than the [horse-drawn] brakes? … Besides, don't preachers travel on Sundays?'

The *Cambrian News* editorialised on the subject in the same issue, pointing out that the Cambrian Railways ran on Sundays, but the Manchester & Milford Railway did not. The Cambrian's operation was accepted, it continued, as was that of the Post Office, of house servants and carriage operators. There was no complaint about preachers who travelled by train or who engaged vehicles on Sundays. It was, the paper thought, a somewhat monstrous doctrine that those who are forced to work every day in the week should have no facilities whatever for enjoyment on Sundays. It would do the ministers of religion no harm if they were not so sure of their congregations every Sunday. The Vale of Rheidol Railway would not run trains if they did not pay and the simple course for the objectors would be not to use them.

Later the paper said that the churches had started a similar 'agitation' some ten years previously, when brake owners ignored it, but the boat owners had complied.

It was flooding at Glanrafon, not the churches, that caused services to be suspended on 5 January 1903, stranding passengers in Aberystwyth. The railway hired charabancs to take them back home. The track was undamaged when the flood subsided, and services resumed the next day.

Capital expenditure to the end of 1902 had reached £62,953. With £51,000 ordinary stock and £16,900 of debentures issued the company was in a position to redeem the £5,000 overdraft. By 21 October 1903 £1,200 of the £2,000 shares surrendered by the Pethick brothers had been sold, realising £1,117 10s which was allocated to the 'contractors' maintenance of permanent way account'. During 1903 some of this money was spent on maintenance leaving £271 15s 10d which was allocated to the maintenance reserve. The remaining £800 was registered to two directors as trustees and the dividend accruing to it was paid to the maintenance reserve too. Construction expenditure is shown in Appendix 4.

Although the railway was deemed to be complete and passenger services had started, there were some issues outstanding raised by the local authorities. The level crossings needed raising, gates on footpath crossings had been padlocked and the road on the harbour branch had not been made good. None of them were resolved without a certain amount of horse trading between the parties. Indeed, the level at Plascrug, near Llanbadarn, was not fully resolved until 1909.

Pethick Brothers also had a long-standing dispute with the town council over the dues charged on rail received at the harbour, first raised in November 1901. The council had reduced its 1s 6d per ton charge by 6d but Pethick Brothers said that this was still much more than they paid at other harbours, generally 6d and sometimes 2d. The council stood its ground but so did the contractor, who refused to pay the £70 bill. In May 1906, saying that the council had no right to charge dues for using the harbour because there was no public

notice of them, Pethick offered 6d per ton in settlement. The council countered with 9d, which seems to have been accepted. An underlying issue was that the harbour cost more to maintain than it earned.

The future of Pethick Brothers' ex-Plynlimon & Hafan Railway Bagnall 2-4-0T came up for discussion at a meeting of the finance committee on 17 February 1903. Smith informed the committee, which had not met during 1902, that the contractors had offered to sell 'Loco *Rheidol*' to the company for £350 and that Bagnall had quoted £97 10s to repair it. When the committee agreed to buy the loco on 24 March the price had increased to £400, £100 payable when the repairs had been completed, on delivery, and two equal instalments at three-month intervals. Some accounts of this loco's history, incidentally, state that it was renamed *Rheidol* after purchase by the company. Smith's reference to it by that name infers that it was so named before the company bought it. The total cost of repairing the loco was £191, including £75 for fitting the automatic vacuum brake. In total it cost £591.

Rheidol, the ex-Plynlimon & Hafan Railway Bagnall 2-4-0T as first running at Aberystwyth, with its spark-arrester chimney and dumb buffers.

Rheidol's chimney was replaced when repairs were made to the locomotive's boiler in 1909. It was photographed on 28 June, soon after it had returned to service. (H.L. Hopwood)

With the railway open, it fell to the *Railway News* (24 January 1903) to compare the journey with what had gone before. Previously, a visit to Devil's Bridge by charabanc could take over five hours and cost more than 5s, the road bypassing the best of the scenery, it claimed. Now, not only did the 12-mile single journey take less time, about an hour, and cost less, 1s 6d return, but the passengers got much better views. It was an up-to-date line, 'only one class has been catered for, everyone gets there in the same time for the same money.' The stations had corrugated iron buildings containing station masters' and ticket offices and waiting rooms.

A few days later, the *Welsh Gazette* (29 January 1903) reported that the railway was making a place for itself in the life of the community and its usefulness was being realised and appreciated more every day. At Capel Bangor the parish was improving and making footpaths to

enhance access to the station, whereas as residents of Cwmystwyth, Pontrhydygroes and Ponterwyd were finding the railway an advantage, saving them time and money. It also reported that the first load of lead ore was transported to the harbour by train on 27 January. The *Cambrian News* (6 February 1903) said that 80 tons of ore had been transported and that it was bound for Antwerp. The ore was stored at the harbour until there was sufficient to ship; in this case it did not leave until June.

Superintendent Rees also saw a 'grand concert' at Aberystwyth's Royal Pier Pavilion on 27 February as an opportunity for the railway. The concert offered performances by Miss Maggie Davies, Prima Donna of Wales, soprano, Madame Juanita Jones, famous Welsh contralto, Mr Thomas Thomas, renowned tenor, Mr Emlyn Davies, famous baritone, and Mr Bertie Ollerhead, the popular violinist. Rees laid on a train that left Aberystwyth at 10.30pm but the venture was probably not as rewarding as he might have hoped, for it appears that it was not repeated.

The chief constable's report to the annual licensing sessions (*Cambrian News* 13 February 1903) had also commented on the railway's impact: The number of persons apprehended and summoned for drunkenness since the licensing sessions on 29 August 1901 was as follows: Apprehended, 139; convicted, 127; discharged, 12; summoned, 28; convicted, 25; discharged, 3. Total number convicted, 152, and total number discharged, 15. The large number of apprehensions for drunkenness was mainly due to the number of men employed on the Devil's Bridge Railway. No comparison can be made with the period before 29 August 1901 because the data was produced in a table which was not published in the newspapers. In 1903 the number of prosecutions for drunkenness fell by 32, because the navvies have left the area, the chief constable reported in February 1904.

There were also criticisms directed at the railway. After a speaker in Manchester had said that he disliked seeing corrugated iron roofs in the country, the *Cambrian News* (27 February 1903) responded, 'So do we. What would [he] say if he went to Devil's Bridge by the Vale of Rheidol Railway, through some of the most beautiful scenery in Wales, and saw that every railway station is roofed with corrugated iron?' On 5 March the *Welsh Gazette* reported that more than half of the corrugated iron carriage shed at Capel Bangor had been blown down in a gale.

Passenger facilities at Capel Bangor had been the subject of criticism in the *Cambrian News* too. The busiest intermediate station, declared the unknown writer, the waiting room was an open shed, exposed to the prevailing weather, pedestrians had to share the cart road which was rutted and dirty, and there were no platforms. Better passenger facilities would result in improved business, the writer claimed.

Capel Bangor, circa 1905. All the main stations had coin-in-the-slot machines. The station master is William Parkins, who originated from, and returned to, the Festiniog Railway. Photographer Arthur John Lewis was 17 years old when the railway was being built in 1902. (A.J. Lewis)

Responsibility for disposing of Pethick Brothers' surplus equipment was taken over by Rees during February, with advertisements for the 8HP engine and saw bench and a large hut, all at Devil's Bridge, and 30 tons of rail, 30-50lb sections, 50 navvy wheel barrows and tool boxes, placed in the *Cambrian News*.

The directorial status quo was disrupted at the general meeting on 26 February 1903, when Cottier's proposal that Frank Ellis be re-elected was countered by W.W. Szlumper's successful proposal that A.H. Pethick be elected instead. Perhaps Ellis saw this coming as he did not attend the meeting. The secretary was instructed to ask him to return 'the gold pass' so that it could be given to Pethick. His shares, £500 ordinary stock, were offered for sale in the *Aberystwyth Observer* on 26 March and he died in 1907.

The resignation of another long-standing director, John Francis, who had been named as one of the promoters in the Act

John Francis, the company's local independent director, died in 1918 and was buried in a prominent position near the east end of All Saint's church at Llangorwen, near Bow Street. James Rees, the manager, is buried near the west end.

of Parliament, was accepted on 19 May. He kept his railway shares until it lost its independence and died in 1918. He was replaced by Joseph Mellowes of the Eclipse Glazing Works in Sheffield.

The company's determination to proceed with the Aberaeron extension was confirmed by the publication of advertisements seeking tenders on 10 March 1903. An 'independent committee' to deal with all matters relating to it was appointed on 19 May, although how independent it could be when it comprised four directors, including the chairman, is impossible to say. £3 3s was payable for copies of the bills of quantities and the specifications and tenders had to be returned by 6 April.

Following site visits in April, 14 tenders had been submitted by 28 May and the lowest, from a 'prominent London firm', provisionally accepted. Rees said that the favoured bid, £47,000, came from a Glasgow firm and that the Pethicks had objected, claiming that their existing investment in the railway deserved preferential treatment, and that the original directors resigned *en masse*, a story that does not fit with known events. Certainly Ellis had been eased out by the Pethicks, but that was before the Aberaeron tenders were sought. Francis might have been unhappy, but he was happy enough to hold onto his shares. Smith stayed for another year. Rees's memory could be inconsistent. He claimed, for example, that two locos were hired from the Festiniog Railway, whereas there was only one.

On 7 May the county council had agreed to advance £18,000 subject to the remainder, £66,000, being subscribed, and appointed David Charles Roberts its nominee director. By 29 October however, the prospects for raising capital seem very familiar: '… bearing in mind the extraordinary financial conditions existing at the present moment in the City and the impossibility which has existed during the last four months of getting public subscriptions to any enterprise …'

Harold Macfarlane, an enthusiast, visited the line in May 1903, travelling with Rees, and submitted his thoughts and observations to *Railway Magazine*. There were six trains daily and two on Sundays, the last still an uncommon feature of train operation in Wales. During Easter week over 1,000 passengers a day had been carried. The railway did good business, he wrote, with merchandise, carrying groceries and parcels, garden produce, eggs and chickens. Three mines were sending 15-20 tons of lead ore per day. Exchange facilities existed with the Manchester & Milford Railway and the increased volume being exported via the harbour because of the railway was responsible for the projected expenditure of up to £15,000 on improvements there.

'Strolling' back to Aberystwyth along the track, Macfarlane found the bracing air made him 'ravenously hungry, and the pleasant olive-green painted stations, though restful to the eye, boasted no refreshment rooms at which he could appease his appetite.' Passengers had to wait three years before they could obtain refreshments on railway premises.

As built, the railway was a mix of the well-specified and the basic. Two locomotives and 12 carriages were enough for two trains with nothing in reserve. The purchase of *Rheidol* was fortuitous. The only intermediate loop, at Capel Bangor, was soon found to be in the wrong place. Where they existed, station facilities were rudimentary, timber framed, corrugated iron-clad buildings. There was nothing at all imposing about either of the railway's terminal stations. Curvature on the harbour branch is the most likely reason the railway never had any bogie wagons.

The *Welsh Gazette* (9 April 1903) reported that over the Easter holiday brakes met the trains at Devil's Bridge, offering conveyance to Pontrhydygroes and Hafod. The following week the paper said that traffic had been extraordinary and that 1,000 passengers had been carried on Good Friday. The railway had also benefitted from an eisteddfod held at Devil's Bridge on Easter Tuesday. William Davies of Cwmystwyth won a prize for his poem, in Welsh, about the railway. Altogether, the *Cambrian News* reported on 17 April, 1,680 passengers were booked during the holiday.

Preparations to cope with increased traffic during the summer had been made, the *Welsh Gazette* said on 28 May. The station approach had been improved and direction signs erected around the town. On 2 April the paper had described how Rees's office had been placed on rollers and moved from one side of the entrance to the other, to improve the layout.

In June 1903 the non-conformist churches renewed their efforts to stop the Sunday trains, also targeting the brakes and petitioning livery stables. In July they targeted visitors directly, distributing printed cards to guest houses and suggesting that they also abstain from attending Sunday concerts. The cards stated that as the railway's directors were strangers to the locality, they were apparently unaware of the area's religious sensibilities. But Rees, who had worked for the Manchester & Milford Railway, would have been aware and if the notion of Sunday working troubled him or the other employees, he would surely have resisted it.

Reporting this matter on 31 July, the *Cambrian News* displayed its usual antipathy towards the churches' position, saying that they wanted a monopoly of Sunday work, and that the greatest Sabbath breaker was Jesus, a fact ignored, it said, by modern Sabbatarians.

In the same issue a reader complained about the effect the railway was having on the businesses of the Aberystwyth posting proprietors (those who hired out horses to visitors) and refreshment providers in the roadside villages. However, David Phillips, one of the proprietors, saw the loss of Devil's Bridge traffic as an opportunity to develop new markets, offering excursions to other scenic places in the area instead.

Aberystwyth station building after it had been rolled across from its original location on the other side of the tracks. The state of *Rheidol*'s smokebox is indicative of it being worked hard. (A.J. Lewis)

Improvements to Capel Bangor station were started in June, an item in the *Cambrian News* noting that a gate and railings had been erected and that the latter and the 'shed' were being painted by the station master. Presumably the shed was the station building or some other structure under the station master's control, painting a building the size of the carriage shed being beyond the capability of a man working on his own.

Along the line, Rhiwfron was added to the list of stations; its construction was mentioned in the *Aberystwyth Observer* on 25 June. 10¾ miles from Aberystwyth, it was located opposite the Rheidol mine, to which it was being connected by means of an aerial ropeway. The paper said that the station would be convenient for residents at Ystumtuen, Bwlchcrwys and Llanfihangel. Druitt submitted a report on the siding there on 26 August 1903. Like the

others, it was controlled by a single lever locked by the tablet.

John M. Henderson & Company of Aberdeen installed the ropeway, with ground works carried out by the mine's own labour. Its span was 1,081ft, the main cables 1,100ft long each, and the anchor bolts 11ft long. At a speed of 260ft per minute, it took 4½ minutes for each 5cwt load to cross and 10 hours to transport 20 tons. The siding held five wagons.

The half-yearly report to 30 June 1903 showed that some three-quarters of the traffic had come from passenger trains, £1,157 16s 8d against £373 5s 10d for merchandise and minerals. An operating profit of £320 17s 1d did not quite equal the debenture interest of £338. No dividend was paid; during construction a 3% dividend had been paid out of capital. During the six months, and one week of 1902, 23,363 passengers had been carried

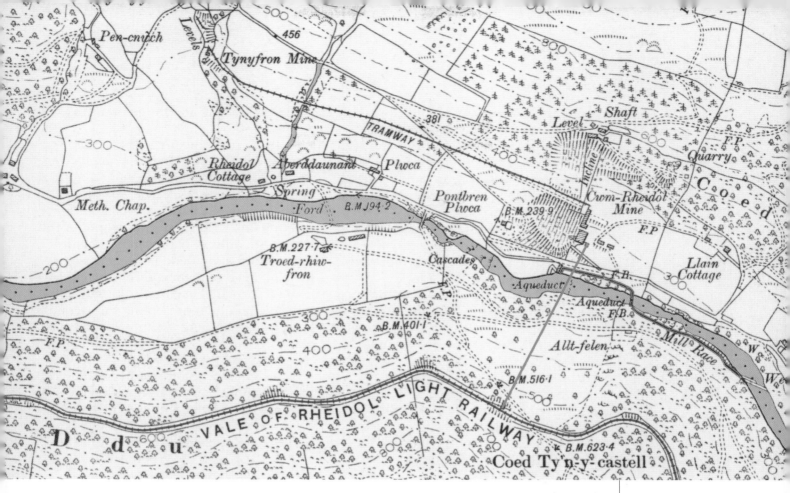

and 13,432 passenger train miles run. Goods and mineral trains had accounted for 3,354 train miles.

Fireman Evan Lloyd Jones sustained a dislocated shoulder when he was crushed uncoupling a wagon during shunting operations on 5 November (*Welsh Gazette* 12 November 1903). Born in Swansea in 1880, he had been one of the firemen on the inaugural trip the year before. He made a good recovery and became one of the railway's drivers, his house in Greenfield Street just a short walk from the loco shed.

In building the railway between the Manchester & Milford Railway bridge and Plascrug, Pethick Brothers had breached the embankment along the riverbank much to the town council's concern, pressing the railway to raise the land. On 26 November 1903 Szlumper wrote to say that the railway was already 2ft 6in higher than shown in the Parliamentary plans. He saw no point in making it higher as the risk was further east, between the river bridge and Llanbadarn. If the council wished to build an embankment along the

Cwm Rheidol seen from Rhiwfron. (A.J. Lewis)

An extract from the 1904 revision of the Ordnance Survey's 6in map of the Rhiwfron area, showing the Cwm Rheidol mine and the cableway that carried lead ore to the railway. (Ordnance Survey)

river there the company would contribute to its cost if the council also obtained contributions from the Cambrian Railways and the affected land owners. Faced with the prospect of building an embankment almost a mile long, eventually the council backed down.

Despite poor weather, the results improved considerably during the second half of 1903. Traffic highlights reported included the transport of 'a large quantity' of timber and the operation of a six-carriage train, both in June. Flooding caused the loss of two trains on 14 August and one on 8 September. Reports of flooding were to be a regular occurrence.

An operating surplus of £1,574 3s was enough to pay the debenture interest in full, to pay a 3% dividend and to place £350 to reserves, leaving £170 13s 4d to be carried forward. Although 79,709 passengers had been carried over 17,576 train miles, merchandise and mineral traffic was only slightly improved, producing £434 5s 5d revenue for train mileage reduced to 2,569 miles.

A recurring feature of the reports under the train mileage heading was an entry for 'ballasting trains', 3,448 miles up to 31 December 1903, no doubt initially reflecting the maintenance avoided by the contractors. The ledger has several entries for wages incurred on 'extra ballasting' in May and June 1903.

The acquisition of the locomotive *Rheidol* was useful in connection with the goods traffic routed onto the harbour branch, Smith reported to shareholders on 8 February 1904, adding that the level of traffic would soon require more wagons. Saying that the passenger traffic could be 'more economically and rapidly carried on' with another station, he added that 'the additional stopping places recently provided' had been worthwhile.

Following a very well-attended general meeting on 24 February 1904, the directors met regularly during the year, attending to a great deal of business. The results of their discussions are summarised, firstly dealing with the directors and the company's administration.

At the general meeting, Madge had been due for re-election but when he was proposed by Smith he said that he was not anxious to be re-elected. His place was taken by N.F. Pethick. At a board meeting on 25 February, Smith announced that as the railway had been built and opened and a dividend paid, he wished to be relieved of the responsibility of being chairman. He would continue as a director though, representing the second-largest shareholding. Arthur Pethick was elected chairman. Mellowes, elected only the previous May, also resigned and was replaced by J.W. Szlumper. Ill-health was to bring about Smith's resignation on 15 June, when he was replaced by another Works Syndicate nominee, Archibald Robert Fowler. Smith died at Bourne End in 1912, aged 55. Whether he was responsible for the offer to sell 'a few' shares published in the *Welsh Gazette* on 3 March 1904 is not known. His estate was valued at £5,095 8s 4d.

Cottier's declaration that from 25 March the board's expenses would be saved was followed by the transfer of the registered office from 28 Victoria Street to 115 Victoria Street, both in Westminster, prompting the secretary's resignation because of the inconvenience; Smith had been paid £250 a year for the use of his office.

The services of C.D. Szlumper as resident engineer had apparently been terminated later in 1903 after he had signed the half-year report's engineers' certificates on 22 July. No explanation was offered for him submitting a claim for £55 10s or for the directors being unwilling to meet it but on 25 February 1904 the newly-elected director Szlumper, his father, offered to pay £10 of the claim personally if the company paid £40, a proposal that was accepted.

C.D. Szlumper also accepted the proposal when the board met again on 29 February, when the possibility of appointing him the company's engineer was discussed. He took up the position from 25 March on a salary of £80 per annum payable quarterly.

Before a decision had been taken he had been asked to report on Rees's proposals to install a passing place at Aberffrwd, forecast by Smith, and a platform at Rheidol Falls. Previously Rees had been instructed to stop a train of a locomotive and six carriages there in fine and wet weather to see if it could be restarted; '… if this was not possible it would be useless having a station at this place.'

Nothing more was said about Rheidol Falls at board level although its existence was reported to shareholders in the half-yearly report. The *Aberystwyth Observer* (3 March 1904) said that it would open on 7 March. Two and a half miles from Aberystwyth, a platform with minimal facilities was opened at Glanrafon on 7 May; it cost £2 11s 2d. The directors were informed that Aberffrwd had been completed on 2 June; Druitt's report was dated 9 June. The tablet instruments had been relocated from Nantyronen. The ground frame had ten levers, including two spare. He required only lighting and a fence to be satisfied; the latter was installed after the platform had been widened. The total cost was £255 7s 10d. The *Cambrian News* (3 June 1904) said that the station had been enlarged because it had turned out to be more profitable than expected.

A level crossing at Plascrug, Aberystwyth, had been criticised by the borough surveyor, who remained unsatisfied even after it had been raised more than 18 inches. In August 1904 J.W. Szlumper said that he had agreed to raise the track to match the level of the adjacent Cambrian line when men were working in the locality. This seems to have been one of several locations where the railway interrupted the area's natural drainage. On 18 October 1904 the *Manchester Guardian* reported that the track had been washed away at Llanbadarn, delaying the 10.00am from Aberystwyth for several hours. Although the afternoon train was cancelled it had been possible to run the 'evening trains', presumably the 6.00pm from Aberystwyth and return.

The plan of the Aberffrwd signalling arrangements submitted to the Board of Trade in 1904. (National Archives)

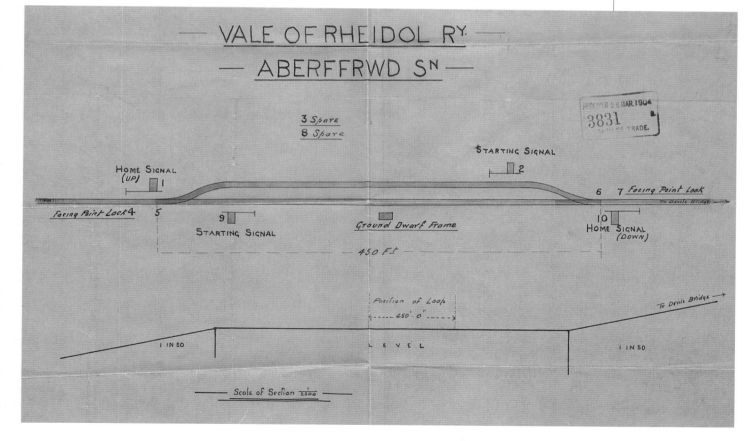

Rheidol's driver oils round at Aberffrwd while waiting for a train to arrive from Devil's Bridge. The ground frame is just out of sight to the left of the photograph. (A.J. Lewis)

C.D. Szlumper's request for 600 new sleepers implies that some of those installed by the contractors had not been of very good quality. He was given permission to buy the six wrought-iron platform seats that he had obtained on approval.

Several carriages required repainting, Szlumper reported in September. Green said that the paint had been affected by the resin in the pitch pine the carriages were built of; as the Capel Bangor carriage shed only held four vehicles, it can be no surprise that paintwork of those left outside soon weathered; in 1920 the shed was described as the 'carriage painting shed'. Approval for two carriages to be painted with one coat of paint and two coats of varnish for £6 each was given in November. The ledger reveals that three carriages and two vans had already been painted at a cost of £31 in June. £13 13s was to be paid for painting two more carriages on 9 October 1905.

During the year locomotive spare parts had been bought, cost £79 4s 6d, and a screwing machine for the workshop. Three wagons had centre couplings attached as an experiment. In November the secretary

reported that Rheidol was 'being overhauled in order that the engineers might prepare a specification of the repairs necessary'. Presumably he meant that it was being dismantled, although why the loco should require any repairs when it had been overhauled the year before is not clear; Green said that the loco required boiler and firebox repairs. Tenders were obtained from the Yorkshire Engine Company, £105; W.G. Bagnall Ltd, £48 10s, and Davies & Metcalfe, £44 15s, the latter being accepted.

Recorded expenditure on Rheidol in 1904 was £2 5s 1d for two new wheels from the Hadfield Steel Foundry Company and £2 17s 7d to the Cambrian for transporting the boiler on 31 December 1904; it cost £3 3s 5d when it was returned in February 1905. Perhaps it was tyres rather than wheels that were replaced. Davies & Metcalfe's bill, £41 10s 10d, was paid on 27 June 1905. B. Loveday, who had painted the carriages, was paid £7 6s 3d for painting the loco, labour only.

Traffic issues that came to the directors' attention during 1904 were mainly to do with special tickets. Rates for annual season tickets from Aberystwyth to intermediate stations were set at: Llanbadarn, £2; Capel Bangor, £6; Nantyronen, £9; Aberffrwd, £10. Rees was also authorised to issue market tickets at reduced rates from 25 March; half-fare season tickets could be issued to pupils of Aberystwyth County School. Groups of at least five passengers were allowed to reserve a compartment providing everyone held a ticket if there were more than five in the compartment. Through bookings from the Cambrian were approved when the larger company agreed to take only 5% commission. Reduced rate tickets, and late trains, had also been offered to those attending a performance of Handel's *Messiah* at Penllwyn, near Capel Bangor, on 16 March.

In April 1904 the directors were concerned that passenger traffic for the year to date was lower than in 1903.

Rees was instructed to bear this in mind and 'do all he possibly could to bring the passenger traffic to what is considered it ought to be.' His earlier request for his post to be designated general manager had been rejected out of hand.

When Rees reported, on 27 August, that coach operators had been spreading rumours that the railway was unsafe the directors took the pragmatic view 'that these matters should be allowed to take their course' while agreeing to consult the solicitor when convenient.

In October the directors took a dim view of Rees's proposal to upgrade the harbour branch for passenger services, asking if he had considered the costs. After reviewing his response, they decided that the time was not right and that he was to do everything possible to promote the Devil's Bridge line to visitors.

A postcard view of the Rofawr wharf, the end of the railway's harbour branch, and the warehouse used to store lead ore before shipment. A Plynlimon wagon has been left outside. The steam ship tied up at the wharf is the Aberystwyth & Aberdovey Steam Packet Company's *Countess of Lisburne*. It traded along the coast as far as Pwllheli before it was sold in 1908. The other vessels have not been identified.

ABERYSTWITH. — THE HARBOUR.

Postal traffic was reviewed in November 1904, Rees having negotiated to carry the mail for £120 per annum, including the operation of one train a day at the company's convenience.

The county council had extended its deadline for contributing to the Aberaeron extension by three months in May 1904. A broker employed to raise the remaining capital, at 2½% commission, explored the possibility of the Cambrian taking on the line's operation, manager C.S. Denniss saying that it would do so if the railway was extended to New Quay and made as standard gauge. When the company's letter saying that 'so far they had been unable to raise the necessary capital for the construction of the Aberystwyth-Aberaeron Railway, but if when times improved they would be able to do so they would have much pleasure in writing again' was read to the county council on 11 August it was greeted with laughter, bringing it to an end. It was probably not unrelated that in February 1905 the Cambrian Railways announced its intention to put two 14-seat motor buses into service between Aberystwyth, Aberayron and New Quay. It was to be 1911 before Aberaeron got its light railway, a standard gauge line to Lampeter.

After allowing for debenture interest, a loss of £226 16s 9d had been made during the first half-year of 1904, revenue being slightly down and expenses increased because track and locomotive maintenance had become the company's responsibility. The situation for the second half-year was much improved, with £1,176 2s available for distribution after payment of debenture interest. Traffic revenue had increased not only because the number of passengers had tripled over the first half but because the return fare had been raised. Compared with the same period in 1903, some 5,000 fewer passengers had been carried, doubtless reflecting a desire to try something new in 1903. A dividend of 3% was declared.

John Pethick, patriarch of Pethick Brothers, had died on 29 March 1904, when a pair of horses that he was driving bolted and his dog cart overturned. He was 76 years old. The *Welsh Gazette* (31 March) claimed that he had been planning to retire to Aberystwyth and that he had a reputation for being reckless. He was buried at Ford Park cemetery, Plymouth, and his estate was valued at £157,310 1s 8d.

A case of apparent vandalism reached the magistrates' court in April, after the permanent way ganger found a rifle bullet in the track, between the rail joints. Three men were charged with intent to cause damage. They had been on the railway but as there was no evidence linking them to the bullet the case was dismissed.

The *Welsh Gazette* was outraged when the town council's annual 'souvenir', a guidebook with advertisements, was published in June. Not only did it direct visitors to one specific outlet to get copies of a specified walking guide, but it said nothing about the railway. The railway had spent £70,000, it expostulated, making the famous Devil's Bridge practically an appendage to the town. It, the railway, was a priceless acquisition for the town and ignoring it in the souvenir was a blunder of such magnitude and stupidity that it passed ordinary understanding.

If they were not before, the booksellers, newsagents and stationers were soon outraged too, petitioning the council to ensure that the 'evil' was not repeated. They were particularly annoyed because the specified guide belonged to a member of the council and the general purposes committee, which was responsible for producing the souvenir.

In May the committee had agreed to replace two old photographs with one of the railway but the publication had been produced by a third party and no-one from the council had seen the proofs. It was agreed to produce slips printed with details of other publications to be inserted.

Despite Rees's efforts to sell Pethick Brothers' plant in 1903, most of it remained unsold. The contractor took charge of it again, commissioning an auctioneer to dispose of it in March 1905. Five 18in gauge steel side-tip Decauville wagons that remained were offered for sale at £4 each on 20 December 1906 (*Welsh Gazette*).

The directors met less often during 1905, their primary interest being the outstanding conveyances for the land taken by the railway. One claim was for loss of crops during construction; starting at £8 19s it was eventually settled for £7 10s. Infrastructure matters dealt with included installing a weighbridge at Devil's Bridge to attract coal traffic and enlarging the Devil's Bridge booking office. Also at Devil's Bridge, the Pethicks acquired the lease on a disused smelting factory to secure a water supply for the railway, the company not being allowed to buy the property although it did pay the £6 annual rent. To improve facilities at the Cambrian transhipment siding, the directors decided to ask for a crane to tranship timber and a

financial contribution towards the cost of a shelter, Rees having claimed that some goods traffic was lost for want of a shelter in bad weather.

Traffic results were varied. Rees reported that Sunday trains between October and Easter had made a loss and was told not to run them from the end of October 1905. In August he was called upon to explain the loss of passenger traffic since 1 July, nearly 5,000 by the end of the year. The directors appeared to be less concerned about their passengers' comfort, leaving Rees's suggestion of installing lavatories at Devil's Bridge in abeyance.

Responding to the directors' question about increased locomotive running costs, Rees explained that wear and tear made them less economical, which the directors accepted. Inadequate maintenance probably also played a part.

Rheidol at Devil's Bridge. The directors did not approve Rees's first application for funding to install water closets at the station.

One of the reasons for lack of directorial activity during 1905 might have been because the Pethicks were trying to offload their investment in the railway to the Cambrian Railways, a process that was to take eight years to bring to fruition. Discussions started following a letter to Denniss on 2 June 1905 suggesting a meeting 'on a matter which we think would be to our mutual interest'. The meeting and an exchange of correspondence took place before they withdrew; 'the scheme … cannot be carried out at the present moment.' Another reason might have been that with the railway in its third year of operation there was simply less for them to do.

The significance of £150 of ordinary shares being offered for sale in Aberystwyth in April 1905 is unknown. They could have been the same 'few' shares offered the year before. Two hundred and fifty shares were offered for sale in the *Cambrian News* on 17 August 1906 and 25 more on 11 January 1907.

An innovation reported by the *Cambrian News* on 4 August was the introduction of saloons by adapting 'a number of ordinary coaches' to meet the 'growing demands of invalids' and others. The directors had accepted Rees's suggestion that the centre compartments of two carriages should be modified to provide 1st class accommodation on 18 April and given approval for the work to be carried out on 27 June. The fixed seats were replaced by reversible seats and chairs made of rattan, as used by the newly-electrified railways in London – Smith's influence, surely? A corridor was created, with two seats on one side and one on the other. The floors were covered with linoleum. Approval to convert a third vehicle was given on 23 August. The alterations cost £45 11s 8d. The fare for travel in these vehicles was set at 3s, double the ordinary fare.

The only additions to rolling stock during 1905 were six box wagons ordered from the Midland Railway Carriage & Wagon Company in June. £252 was paid for them on 14 November. The *Welsh Gazette* reported their arrival two days later, saying that they had a larger capacity than those already in use and were 'provided with side doors and other conveniences for the easier handling of traffic.'

The concept of bridal parties including a distinctive rail journey in their nuptial arrangements is clearly nothing new. On 12 August the *Montgomeryshire Echo* described a wedding in Llanidloes, saying, 'the wedding party subsequently drove together with a number of friends to Devil's Bridge, where they entrained for Aberystwyth by the miniature Rheidol Valley railway.'

A train was delayed for two hours on 18 August, when a bullock got on the track and was run down by the loco, which was derailed. The driver, Robert Davies, who had been a fireman in 1902, was slightly injured, said the *Cambrian News*, and the animal was killed. Another report on 25 August said that the train concerned was the 3.15pm from Devil's Bridge. Several animals from Pwllcanawen Farm, near Capel Bangor, had got onto the line and a permanent way ganger was about to herd them back into the field when the train came. 'Unfortunately the driver did not appear to have noticed the animals,' observed the paper.

Always on the lookout for ways to draw attention to the railway, during 1905 Rees obtained permission from the town council to erect a flagstaff near the station entrance, rent 1s a year, and a sign, 12ft x 2ft, on the wall of the 'old weighing shed', rent 5s. The year before, the council had approved the pasting of 'pictorial posters' on a wall near to the station. In 1906 he obtained a £10 contribution towards the cost of distributing the poster, which promoted both the town and the railway and opened a booking and enquiry office by the pier (*Welsh Gazette* 5 April and 19 July). The latter was run until 1909, the council refusing Rees's offer to renew the tenancy for £5 in 1910.

In January 1906 the directors discussed the reduction in goods traffic being carried, Rees explaining that it was due 'in some degree' to decreased output. He had, however, made arrangements to tranship timber with the Cambrian and that traffic was about to start. By 5 May revenue from this source had reached £88 11s 11d. In 1944 Rees told W.E. Hayward that wagons were used as bolsters to carry timber up to 60ft long, the trains travelling at a crawl.

Rees also told Hayward that at its peak the ore traffic was enough for the wagons to have to make two return trips in a day. Most was destined for smelting works at Padeswood, via the Cambrian, and Swansea via the Manchester & Milford Railway. Some ore was exported via the harbour to Antwerp and iron or sulphur pyrites to Nobel's works at Arklow, Ireland. Back traffic was usually coal, lime and merchandise.

Thanks to a little bit of horse-trading, it was in 1906 that Rheidol Falls and Rhiwfron got their waiting shelters. The Rheidol Mining Company agreed to let the company have the land it needed for a shelter at Rheidol Falls providing the company erected a shelter at Rhiwfron. The directors agreed on 31 January.

The General Post Office had made a unilateral change to the fee payable for the carriage of mails early in 1906, eventually offering £40 annually to be paid via the Railway Clearing House. The company held out for more, settling for £60 for a minimum of two years in June 1906.

C.D. Szlumper was given a two-year contract from 30 June 1906. During the year he reported on a rock fall of some 300 tons half a mile from Devil's Bridge, which cost £1 18s 3d to tidy up, and proposed improvements to the culvert at Aberffrwd. He had also gained approval to buy five tons of new rail.

Three years after the lack of refreshments was first mentioned, a confectionery stall was set up at Devil's Bridge, earning the company £2 rental. This was quickly followed by the establishment of a W.H. Smith & Son bookstall there too, the company receiving 5% of its revenue. When the Hafod estate objected to the stall in March 1907 the company replied that the usage was not in contravention of the land's conveyance.

An attempt to derail a train on 17 September 1906 derailed the loco's pony truck. The *Cambrian News* said that a stone had been jammed in the rails and that the train continued some way before the driver realised that anything was amiss. The culprit was not identified.

The possibility of selling the railway to the Cambrian arose again on 6 July 1906, with a letter to Denniss from J.W. Szlumper asking for a meeting at which Smith would be present. Following the meeting, Szlumper confirmed the offer on 20 July: the debenture interest to be guaranteed and the line worked for 55% of the gross receipts with a minimum rent of 3% on the £51,000 ordinary stock. At a meeting on 16 October Denniss rejected the proposal as absurd. The guarantee was £2,206 yet the net revenue in 1904 had only been £1,739 and in 1905, £1,495, an evaluation that seemed to catch the Rheidol party unawares, Denniss told a Cambrian director. After 'considerable' discussion the meeting broke up with the Aberystwyth contingent going away to consider Denniss's best offer, to guarantee the debenture interest and to work the railway for 65% of the receipts. On 2 November the Pethicks countered with 60% 'on the understanding that the gross earnings do not fall below the average of the three years ending 31 December 1906'. Denniss rejected this and the Pethicks again withdrew.

Despite this, the Cambrian continued to work on the proposal, getting reports on the rolling stock and permanent way in December 1906. The locomotive superintendent said that he did not think that the locomotives had been maintained as they should have been. The 'larger engines' had not had any boiler or firebox work done on them since they were built, they were run down, dirty and neglected. The one he saw working was knocking badly. *Rheidol*, in better condition, was used on ballast trains and 'very light' passenger trains.

The carriages seemed in fair condition but he could not see the bogies to assess them. The paint was deteriorating. The loco shed had holes in its roof and was in poor condition. There were few spares and few tools. One of the drivers had been a fitter and occasionally did shed repairs. A joiner did what he could for the carriages and wagons and also did repairs to station buildings. More serious locomotive repairs, he said, had been carried out at the former Davies & Metcalfe foundry; this had been bought by the MMR and taken over by the GWR, which leased the Manchester & Milford Railway from 1 July 1906. It was being closed on 12 December, the day of the visit; he did not know where loco repairs would be carried out in future.

The engineer said that 'the general condition of the road is good and it has been well maintained'. The rail was in excellent condition, very little worn, apparently about 52lbs/yard. There were different sections by different makers, with 1885 and 1895 dates noted. A short

distance had much lighter rail, probably not more than 40 or 45lbs. There was ample siding room at Aberystwyth, Capel Bangor and Devil's Bridge, a single short siding at Nantyronen and Rhiwfron and the exchange siding at Plascrug.

The sleepers were uncreosoted, of larch and other native timber, and were sawn roughly out of small trees. They were in good condition. The rails were fastened with dog spikes, iron clips and coach screws. The ballast was fairly good, there was plenty of it.

Denniss had submitted a detailed report to the traffic and works committee on 5 December 1906. He liked the idea of taking on the railway, if only to stop the GWR getting it and diverting the exchange traffic to the Manchester & Milford route. The Cambrian could save on management costs and on the railway's winter mileage, he explained. Working the Welshpool & Llanfair Light Railway cost 59% of receipts and he saw no reason why the Rheidol should not be comparable. It needed

Rheidol and *Edward VII* at Nantyronen. The water tank was erected in 1903/4 at a cost of £23 8s 9d.

developing though, and its shareholders would have to provide the capital.

On 21 December he wrote to the Pethicks again, stating at the outset that he could not accept their proposal. The track was not satisfactory, some rail was more than 20 years old, sleepers were of inferior quality, the rolling stock was far from satisfactory, the locomotives were run down and the carriages were of slight construction and needed money spending on them. The cost of putting the railway into good order must be considered when calculating the railway's worth.

The Cambrian would work it for 70% of receipts for the five years, followed by 65%, the difference paying for the refurbishment. It would undertake to develop the railway 'reasonably'. Capital expenditure would only be incurred with the owning company's consent; if the Cambrian found such capital because the owners could not it would be recouped from any balance of gross receipts above working expenses and attract interest at 4%. The Cambrian could use any surplus land. Any rights attaching to the Aberaeron light railway order would be transferred to the Cambrian. The agreement would be for 99 years or in perpetuity subject to review on a decennial basis. Denniss applied pressure by stating he wanted to put the proposals to the Cambrian directors when they met early in January, that the matter could not be left in abeyance, and that if the proposal was not accepted by the end of December it must be considered withdrawn. Perhaps not surprisingly, the Pethicks rejected it on 2 January 1907.

There was another meeting that found little common ground. Denniss made a further report to the traffic and works committee on 13 February 1907, urging that a way should be found to reach an agreement otherwise the GWR might make an agreement to take the railway's exchange traffic, worth about £1,000 a year, to the Cambrian. A final meeting took place on 20 February, when Denniss offered to guarantee the debenture interest; 'after further conversation it was understood that the negotiations were at an end.'

Transhipment at Plascrug			
Year	Lead ore	Blende ore	Revenue to Cambrian
1903	13t 10c		£5 3s 5s
1904	16t	1,321t 13c	£362 10s 9d
1905	260t 11c	2,684t 11c	£717 8s 6d
1906 (six months)	150t 19c	977t	£261 15s 4d

The Pethicks must have tried to dispose of their Rheidol interest elsewhere, for on 14 May 1907 Denniss received a letter from an intermediary, 'a friend of mine has the option', offering 42,750 shares at 6s and the debentures at £4 10s. Offering the debentures at this price must have been an error. The offer seems to have been ignored.

William Hughes had issued a summons against the company in September 1906, alleging damage to his cattle due to defective fencing. Such claims were usually settled by Rees out of petty cash, in the previous three years ranging from 10s and £1 5s for lambs to 10s for one sheep, £1 5s 6d for two sheep and £8 for a bullock killed (the one run down on 18 August 1905? Hughes was probably the farmer concerned.) Other claims dealt with included 9s for a lost sack of oatmeal, 12s 6d for lost corn and £5 19s for damage to a horse. The only claim by passengers was in September 1906 when 9s was paid after a connection with the Cambrian had been missed.

Officers at the Board of Trade appeared somewhat baffled in May 1907 when Rees asked if explosives could be carried in one of the railway's vans. In response to traders' demand, he wrote, he wished to carry occasional consignments, not exceeding two tons, about six times a year. The van he proposed to use was strongly constructed, with 2½ inch thick floor plates and lined with ⅛in sheet iron plate, iron sheeting covering the ⅜in boards used on the roof. Receiving approval, he would have the words 'GUNPOWDER VAN' painted on the vehicle's sides in bold letters.

He was informed that he should refer to the model bylaws prescribed by the 1875 Explosives Act and ensure that there was no exposed iron or steel in the interior of any vehicle used, which rendered the railway's vehicle unsuitable unless it was lined. Rees had the bylaws adopted, undertook to comply with them, and asked for copies in order to have them printed for display at stations. Despite this, there is no evidence that the railway ever carried any explosives.

Some of the land purchase claims dragged on for a long time, those of Ann Morgan over land near the river at Llanbadarn being particularly troublesome. At Aberystwyth only half of the £800 purchase price of council land there had been paid. In 1907 the company agreed to pay interest on the outstanding balance at 3¼% less tax from the date of possession until 31 March 1907 and then at 4%.

When he was asked to account for a decline in receipts in March 1907 Rees explained that it was due to the withdrawal of the 10.00am from Aberystwyth, cancelled as an economy measure on board instructions the previous November. Having chosen the cancelled train Rees was presumably aware of the likely outcome.

It is difficult to form an opinion on the relationship between Rees and the directors. They refused to allow him to take the title of general manager when that was the function he performed, his request for a pay rise was refused, he was rarely invited to attend their meetings, and they were quick to jump if they thought he was acting beyond his status. On the other hand, he appeared to have a free hand on staffing levels and pay, subjects that were never mentioned in the minutes. It may be just the secretary's intervention in recording his, Rees's, reports that sometimes gives the impression that he took advantage of their remoteness from the railway to give the directors less than helpful information.

Consideration of Rees's May 1907 proposal to acquire two open carriages was 'adjourned' on 28 January 1908. Also on that date, Szlumper's report on couplings was adjourned until Rees could attend a London meeting. Considering a letter from him on 14 February, the directors agreed to a trial on a short train at £1 15s per carriage. How these couplings differed from those already in use is not known.

Six years after the railway had been opened the financial position was becoming critical. The capital account was £2,267 3s 6d overspent, that amount being a liability on the revenue account, and although the debenture interest had been paid dividends had never reached 2%. An overdraft, £704 2s 3d in 1908, was required during part of the year and the debentures were due to be redeemed on 1 January 1908. The revenue and construction reserves, nearly £1,000 together, were to be transferred to the capital account in 1908.

When it came to dealing with the debentures, the Pethicks refused to accept new ones, agreeing to accept a two-year extension instead. Their subsequent transfer to the Eagle Insurance Company went unrecorded.

On 28 January 1908 the secretary reported that an overdraft of £750-£1,000 would be required to cover the debenture interest in July; the bank had agreed if the directors gave personal guarantees. Cottier resigned as a director on 2 April, possibly as a consequence of being asked to give a guarantee; he had not attended a meeting since 25 February 1904.

In March 1908 the Aberystwyth town clerk complained about the harbour branch, asking the company to have the area between the rails paved with granite setts. The council rejected the directors' offer to carry out the work if they paid half of the £35 estimated cost.

When a 9-hole golf course was opened behind the Hafod Arms Hotel, within a few hundred yards of Devil's Bridge station, in June 1908, its owner asked for cheap weekend tickets. Rees could not see any benefit for the company, especially as it was a private venture and especially not in August and the directors agreed with him. However, Rees returned with a proposal to

Aberystwyth, Arrival at Devils Bridge Station.

issue combined rail and golf day tickets for 2s 6d, of which the railway would take the standard 1s 6d fare. This was accepted.

Another joint venture that came to fruition at the same time was a combined rail and coach tour from Aberystwyth to Hafod via Devil's Bridge. The fare was 3s, the company receiving 1s 6d plus 10% of the balance.

A combined board meeting and inspection took place on 6 July 1908. Having inspected the harbour branch the directors thought that it would be pointless trying to make a satisfactory roadway unless the quay wall was raised to the same height. A copy of Szlumper's report was sent to the town clerk who passed it on to the public works committee. Ultimately no action was taken despite the council's insistence that the company was liable.

The locomotive water supply at Aberffrwd was obtained from an adjoining landowner at a cost of £3 a year. Szlumper suggested that installing a hydraulic ram would be cheaper and arrangements were made with another landowner to install a ram to supply the water at a cost of 5s a year.

Rees returned to the subject of open carriages, suggesting that two goods wagons could be converted for seasonal use. Szlumper was to enquire of the Board of Trade if such vehicles could be run without vacuum brakes. If he did make the enquiry no trace has been found of it, or of the Board's response, but it was not likely to have been in the affirmative.

Nevertheless, two wagons were put into service during August. The first reported use of them was in May 1909 (*Welsh Gazette* 27 May) when a party of journalists representing London and provincial newspapers visited the town and enjoyed a trip to Devil's Bridge in one of them. Green (see bibliography) asserts that they were equipped with vacuum brakes, but given their small size this seems unlikely and no brake pipe is visible on the one photograph known to the author that shows the end of one of them (above). The practice of running them at the end of the train, attached to the brake van, is also indicative that they were not equipped. These conversions never featured in the rolling stock returns.

A busy scene at Devil's Bridge as a newly-arrived trainload of passengers heads for the falls. The train includes two of Rees's semi-open conversions and the adapted wagons are stabled in the siding. (Frank Phillips Series)

Devil's Bridge Train, Rheidol Valley, near Aberystwyth.

A double-headed train at Cwm yr Ogos with the third semi-open conversion in the train and two wagon conversions tagged onto the end.

Rees told W.E. Hayward that the open carriages were so popular that he charged 3d extra to travel in them. They were attached to the rear of the train to place their occupants as far from the smell and dust of the locomotives as possible (*Cambrian News* 13 August 1909).

More attempts were made to interest the Cambrian in the railway in June and July 1908. By now the debentures and ordinary shares (40,000 in June, 42,250 in July) were on offer for £27,000. To one Denniss replied that the Cambrian had already considered the railway and he would not care to put it before the directors again. The other offer had been made to Davies, a Cambrian director, who asked Denniss about it. Sending the correspondence and reports, Denniss explained that Pethick Brothers had been rebuffed by the GWR and doubted that

it would ever be possible to agree on a valuation.

Passenger traffic and revenue in 1908 were reduced compared with 1907, although mineral traffic was slightly increased. On 26 August the directors called upon Rees to attend the next board meeting, in the meantime to report on Sunday trains, winter traffic, opening the sides in some of the existing carriages and running circular tours.

Discussing the report on 6 October, the directors immediately ruled against the circular tours. Two carriages were to be converted and the Sunday and winter services were to be continued as previously. Work on converting the carriages was to be started straightaway; the estimated cost was £34 18s each.

C.D. Szlumper submitted a detailed report on 23 November 1908, saying that although the track was in good condition (another) five tons of new rail was required 'without delay'. Unspecified precautionary measures were needed to protect the railway at the river bridge. Authority was given to purchase the rail while the river bridge was to be dealt with in the most economical manner.

The fall in traffic in 1908 was followed by a slight improvement in 1909 and then three years of very good figures, the best of the railway's independent existence. Costs were contained too, so the improvement translated to the bottom line if not to dividends. From an operating perspective the railway appeared to be a successful undertaking, with its ratio of expenditure to receipts always less than 80%, but this was at the expense of carrying around £1,000 of unpaid bills on the balance sheet for several years. The conversion of three wagons to carry timber during the second half of 1907 and 1908 appears to have been temporary; the status quo was resumed in the following half-year's report.

Magistrates heard two cases affecting the railway during 1909. The first resulted in Mary Edwards being fined 1s and costs for trespassing on the railway between her home at Rheidol Cottage and Llanbadarn on 4 February. Rees told the magistrates that she had been warned repeatedly but would not desist. She did not appear in court. Her route was the section of track where the train had been derailed in 1906.

The second concerned Jenkin Arthur Jenkins, a farmer's son, who had been charged with travelling with intent to avoid payment, heard on 25 March 1909. He said that he had no money so travelled with an unused ticket that he had bought 12 months before. After the station master and a guard gave evidence that Jenkins had offered to pay, the company's solicitor said that the company did not wish to press the charge, which resulted in a 6d fine and 14s costs for Jenkins. Given that the evidence that he had offered to pay was accepted, it is difficult to understand why the charge

of 'intent to avoid' was brought, or why it was proceeded with.

The case did not act as a warning to H.W. Morgan who was caught travelling from Aberystwyth to Capel Bangor without a ticket in November. When Rees reported that this was the third time Morgan had travelled with an invalid ticket in two years the directors resolved to start proceedings against him, but Morgan's apology was sufficient to prevent action being taken.

There was personal success for Rees on two fronts on 5 May 1909, for the directors not only agreed to giving him an increase in salary of £20, his first since appointment, but they also agreed to his position being that of general manager, with duties and powers remaining unchanged.

The bank manager was obviously becoming concerned about the railway's financial health, for on 23 July 1909 the secretary reported that 'he had interviewed the manager of the National Provincial Bank at Aberystwyth and had made satisfactory arrangements in connection with the company's account for the current half year.' Considering that he had to travel from London to Aberystwyth for the 'interview', that sounds more as if he had responded to a summons to attend.

When the directors visited Aberystwyth on 30 August 1909, they inspected one of the original carriages that had been converted into a semi-open; it had retained its original sides and doors. The concept had first been considered in October 1908. The cost was £34 18s plus a £9 overspend. Satisfied, they told Rees to have two more ready for the 1910 season.

This trespass sign is displayed in the Narrow Gauge Railway Museum at Tywyn.

Seen in 1910, when *Edward VII* was newly repainted in this ornate livery and the second of Rees's semi-open conversions, the third vehicle in this short train, had just entered service. Beyond the end of the train, carriages can be seen in the Cambrian station. (Kingsway Series)

The passengers in No 11, the first of the semi-open conversions, which had been converted in 1909, pose for the photographer.

Train in the Rheidol Valley.

The directors also considered the desirability of extending the railway up to the main line station at Aberystwyth, shared with the GWR and the Cambrian. Szlumper produced a plan and an estimate but it was necessary to determine that the GWR's compulsory purchase powers over the land required had expired; the railway could not obtain powers to use it if the GWR already had them to use it for its own purposes.

Asked to devise means of reducing the expense of winter operating, Rees suggested obtaining a 'petrol car', saying that it would not only save money but would increase revenue. On 3 November 1909 Szlumper reported the Rheidol Foundry's owner telling him that such a vehicle would cost up to £700 and would not cope with the railway's gradients. This was the right judgement for the time and Rees was probably in advance of the market making the suggestion. A quote of £600 for a petrol locomotive was obtained from an unidentified manufacturer in 1910. The directors offered to pay £300 after a six-month trial and the remainder after a further three months but in May decided that an experiment was not justified.

One of the reasons for the 'enthusiasm' for a petrol loco might have been a problem with *Rheidol*. The loco had been mentioned in one of Szlumper's reports and discussed by the directors without any explanation being recorded. Having refused to proceed with a petrol loco, consideration was given to 'a small steam locomotive' on offer from Bagnall, until Szlumper reported, on 6 June, that the summer traffic could be worked by the existing fleet. When Szlumper obtained quotations for *Rheidol*'s repair in October 'the matter was referred to the chairman'.

A 'misfortune of bargain hunting' was the reason that Rees lost a court claim to recoup the 10s spent on a second-hand grass mowing machine that turned out to be 'worthless' in October 1909 (*Aberystwyth Observer*). Examination of the previous owner, who Rees sued, revealed that it had been purchased through a third party, which led to the judge finding in favour of the defendant and making the comment. Rees should have sued the third party.

The reductions in the winter timetable resulted in a comment in the *Cambrian News* (5 November 1909) to the effect that

Rheidol and its short train at Cwm yr Ogos circa 1906.

DEVIL'S BRIDGE RAILWAY AT DEVIL'S BRIDGE, 69608

A 1911 scene at Devil's Bridge. The second train has just arrived, and its passengers set off to see the falls. Two Plynlimon & Hafan Railway wagons and a bolster wagon are visible beyond the goods shed. (James Valentine)

it would have an impact on the valley's inhabitants' movements. The paper understood that the winter passenger traffic was insufficient to pay for more trains and that the mineral traffic was also low because of reduced demand.

Expenditure during 1909/10 included £13 19s 7d on boiler tubes in two batches, £58 3s 9d on rail, two batches, £23 14s 6d for vacuum brake fittings, £4 13s 9d for wheels from Hadfield & Company, and £15 8s to the Expanded Metal Company [for wire mesh] for the open cars. Lightfoot, the painter, appeared several times in the lists of payments made. Not explained were payments totalling £24 16s to the Midland Railway Carriage & Wagon Company with the description 'wagons' attached.

Rees secured a reduction of 6d per ton on the harbour dues in respect of 25 tons of rail shipped from Liverpool in October, and also obtained £2 14s 4d from the council towards the cost of advertising the railway, which was considered to benefit the town.

Aberystwyth station was burgled on 21 January 1910. The culprit turned out to be a 21-year-old miller from Yorkshire,

who had gained entry though an open window and broke open three drawers to steal 2s 3d in cash, nine 1d postage stamps and four keys. He pleaded guilty, saying that he had borrowed money from his girlfriend and wanted to repay her. After his mother made 'a piteous appeal' (*Cambrian News* 11 February) for leniency he was bound over on his own recognisance for £20 plus costs. The chairman of the bench said that they were sorry for his mother. Their faith was justified, for the guilty party served in the Royal Army Service Corps during the First World War, earning the Victory and British war medals, and married in 1918.

When the debentures matured again in 1910, the Eagle Insurance Company refused to convert them to debenture stock, agreeing instead to them being extended for five years. The most likely explanation for the insurance company's interest in the debentures is that it was holding them as security for advances made to Pethick Brothers.

In July 1910 the railway removed the Manchester & Milford Railway exchange siding, much to the consternation of the

With the Territorials at Aberystwyth. August. 1912.

The Territorials' camp at Lovegrove in 1912. The railway is on the far side of the river. (Baxter's)

local GWR manager who pressed for its reinstatement. Establishing that there was no contractual obligation to maintain it, the directors refused. Whether the siding's removal was a deliberate act on the part of the directors in the knowledge that the Cambrian might take over the line or was just a coincidence, there is no way of telling.

Now that he had his general manager title, Rees wanted the same conditions as his fellow officers, to have the security of a three-year contract. On 6 July 1910 he was given one that expired in June 1912, the same as the others. He had experienced a personal tragedy in March, with the death of his wife Sophia from appendicitis, leaving him with four children aged between 10 and 2½ to bring up. He married Phoebe Selina Williams in 1921.

The first of several training camps run by the Welsh Territorial Division was operated in 1910, based at Lovesgrove on the opposite site of the river from the railway, near to Capel Bangor. Giving details of the camps – there was another at Bow Street – the *Cambrian News* (25 March 1910) said that a bridge would be put over the river

to enable the men to relax in Aberystwyth after a day on manoeuvres.

With 14,000 troops participating, the 1910 camp ran from 24 July until 7 August and Rees installed a temporary station, installing a loop using unused track from Aberystwyth according to Green (see Bibliography), and running extra trains which earned £375 14s 11d against expenditure of £103 10s 1d. Afterwards he told the directors that the camp's commanding officer had said how satisfied he had been with the railway's service, and suggested that as he (Rees) had taken on extra work and responsibilities he should be paid an honorarium, receiving £12 12s for his pains. One exercise had involved, incidentally, the concept of a revolt in Ireland being followed by a landing of forces north of Aberystwyth, the defending troops fighting a rearguard action and using the railway as cover.

The harbour branch came back on the agenda in August 1910 after the council submitted a bill for £9 9s for nine years rental of the right of way saying that there was an agreement that the borough accountant had overlooked. The secretary being unable to find any evidence of such an agreement, the council was asked to supply a copy. It was not mentioned again.

On 9 March 1909 Rees had attempted to interest David Davies MP, grandson of the famous Welsh contractor and a Cambrian Railways director, in buying the railway. Although he thought that the railway was about to be sold, he had written, he thought that Davies might be drawn to it, adding that if the electrification scheme that he had been investigating was put into effect the return could be as much as 6%. If Davies did reply his response was not retained.

Among the papers is an undated and unsigned briefing note passed to the Cambrian Railways' traffic manager, Charles Leonard Conacher, by Davies's office in June 1910 although almost certainly not written by him. Referring to Rees's electrification proposal it states that Siemens had estimated £4,800 for six motor coaches and £4,750 for 'overhead equipment and material' to which a handwritten comment, 'can be done cheaper', had been appended. At 1d per unit, the maximum annual cost of working an 'efficient' service would be less than £500. Assuming savings in locomotive operation and maintenance, maintaining previous business and carrying 'lost' passengers, a rather crude calculation showed the balance available for distribution to shareholders and servicing debt would be more than doubled.

The anticipated 15,000 participants in the Territorial camp and 11,000 attending a forthcoming National Union of Teachers' conference made the future look even rosier. Apart from the comment referred to in the next paragraph nothing more was to be said about electrifying the railway.

Of the railway, the report states that with only three locomotives there were long intervals between trains, the engines were old and only capable of light loads, it had always been impossible to cope with heavy traffic at peak times, 'compulsory sacrifice of passengers affected the revenue … while uncomfortable crowding in stuffy compartments diverted a considerable number of passengers to the road brakes.' Other factors were the Aberystwyth station's location, a mile from the Marine Parade, and the irregular running of trains. This last was undoubtedly a consequence of trying to accommodate both local and tourist demands. As two of the locos were less than ten years old and the third not much older, the comment about them suggests that maintenance was not as good as it might have been. A note on the report suggested bidding £29,000 for the Pethick shares and debentures and allowing £10,000 for electrification.

Following some investigations carried out during June, Conacher had submitted a report to the Cambrian directors on 11 July 1910. The offer of all the debenture stock and £42,000 ordinary stock had been made to Alfred Herbert, a Cambrian director, initially for £29,500, now reduced to £23,250. A few days previously, £3,350 ordinary shares, the syndicate's, had been offered at 25% by a Swansea broker. The syndicate had entered voluntary liquidation in January 1910, unable to continue its business 'by reason of its liabilities'.

Conacher had been presented with two scenarios supporting the concept of the Cambrian taking over the railway, protecting the company against a competitor using it to develop a competing route into Aberystwyth and as a means of strengthening the Cambrian's position in relation to the competitive Vale of Rheidol traffic. The topography made the former unlikely, he thought; such competition was more likely to arise if the East & West Wales Railway's 1898/9 schemes for a railway from Kington through Rhayader to connect with the Manchester & Milford Railway was revived.

In his opinion, if the offer was to be pursued it should be on the basis of whether the stock could be bought to make a return. He thought that an average profit of £1,250 could be assumed, and on that basis forecast a return of 4¾% on

the £23,250 offer price. A further benefit would be the guaranteed retention of the exchange traffic, most of which was routed via the Cambrian. 'One of our colleagues,' he wrote, 'is willing to contribute in a substantial degree if others … will join in,' on the basis that the railway would be merged into the Cambrian as soon as it was convenient.

The directors moved quickly, with Davies, Thomas Craven, Alfred Herbert, Charles Bridger Orme Clarke and John Conacher, chairman and C.L. Conacher's father, participating in the purchase, the first taking the largest share. Only one of them, Herbert Stern, Baron Michelham, objected, saying that the valuation was too high and that the figure given for average profits misrepresented them as they had declined every year from 1903. Subsequently, Herbert's company, Herbert Brothers, bought the syndicate's shares.

A final view of the railway in the last days of its independence. Close examination of the photograph reveals that the train is mixed, with several wagons attached to it. (Photochrom)

ROLLING STOCK GALLERY 1902-88

No 1 *Edward VII* at Aberystwyth circa 1912. The timber plank had been bolted to the buffer beam to ensure that the loco had less far to fall if it was derailed. A semi-open conversion is stabled beyond the loop crossover.

No 2 *Prince of Wales*, a poor-quality image but it is a good representation of the loco as delivered.

No 3 *Rheidol* with the dumb buffer and spark-arrester chimney that it had retained from its brief time on the Plynlimon & Hafan Railway.

No 3 returning to Aberystwyth during the Cambrian era. At some point its pony-truck wheels had been changed for spoked examples. (K.A.C.R. Nunn)

No 7 on shed, with steam heating train connector removed. This loco has no tankside grab handles when built.

No 8 in the 1926 station on 31 August 1937, still equipped with steam heating.

No 1213 still in GWR livery at Aberystwyth on 25 August 1948.

No 7 in the variant of GWR livery applied around the time of Nationalisation.

No 8 in its first BR livery.

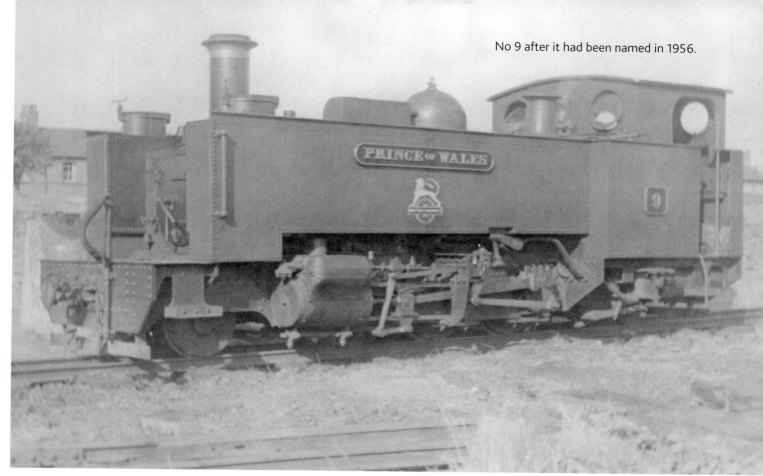

No 9 after it had been named in 1956.

No 9 in its 1957 livery.

A good view of the top of No 9 at Devil's Bridge.

No 9 freshly painted in BR blue, taking water at the new Aberystwyth station in 1968. (David Mitchell)

No 7 when the blue livery has worn a little. It has a minor difference in the positioning of the double-arrow logo compared with No 9 in the previous picture.

A nice portrait of No 7 in its blue lined-out livery taking water from the standard gauge water crane in 1978.

No 8 was the first loco to be turned out in 'historic livery' in BR days, although only No 9 is thought to have carried this version. Seen approaching Llanbadarn in 1981.

No 9 painted in a representation of the livery applied to No 2 in 1902.

No 7 on 17 May 1983, its first day in the sponsored 1957 livery.

No 8 in Cambrian livery in 1986.

No 7 in the 1983 livery at Aberffrwd, after the loop had been reinstated post-privatisation. (Peter Heath)

No 7 on shed in 1992. By this date, the smokebox door numberplate brackets had been removed.

The third semi-open carriage conversion and one of the wagon conversions at Devil's Bridge circa 1912. Behind the bogie carriage one of the Plynlimon & Hafan wagons has been painted in the railway's livery. (A.J. Lewis)

The first of the semi-open carriage conversions as running under GWR ownership.

The third semi-open had been modified slightly by the time it was photographed during the GWR era. (H.F. Wheeller)

No 4998, one of the 1923 batch of summer cars. Safety bars were fitted in 1924. (GWR)

No 4149, the first of three 1938-built summer cars, in September 1950. The square mesh distinguish these from the 1923 stock, which has diamond mesh.

A line of GWR stock in the 1950s. From the left: a brake composite, two brake vans, a 3rd open and two summer cars.

One of the 1923 summer cars in green livery.

No 2, one of
the railway's
original carriages,
photographed by the
GWR in 1922. (GWR)

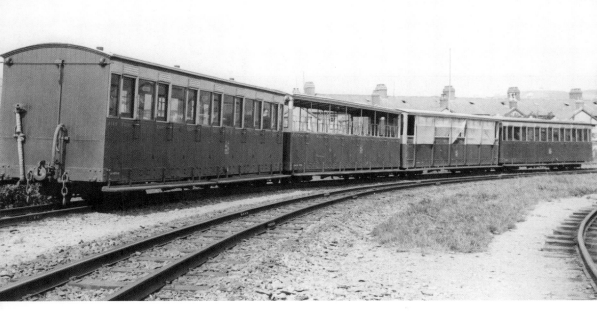

With a 1923 summer car second from right, three original carriages are seen in GWR livery stabled at
Aberystwyth. The closed carriages were equipped with steam heating in 1924.

No 137, one of the original brake vans, equipped with steam heat and painted in GWR livery. These three vehicles were condemned on 30 April 1948. (G.F. Parker)

One of the three 1938 brake vans at Devil's Bridge still in GWR livery circa 1950. (David Elliott)

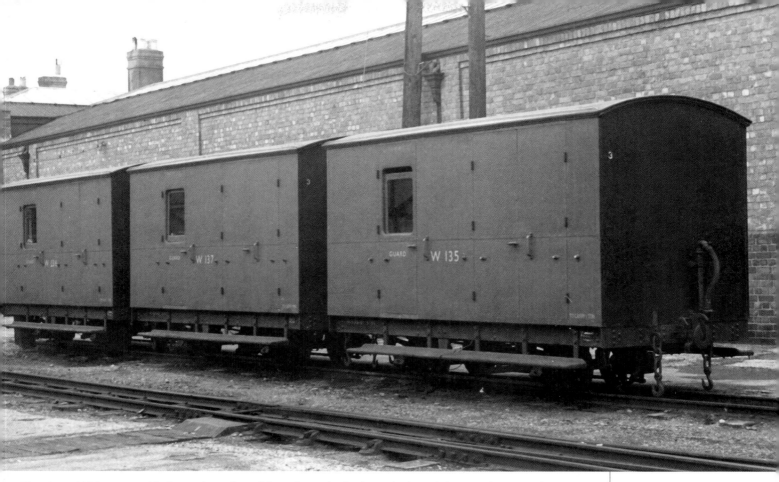

The three 1938 vans stabled together. They did not have the lookout ducket of their predecessors but were fitted with windows in their downhill ends instead.

Van No 137 painted in GWR livery in 1985.

Still in GWR livery, and weathered by outdoor storage during the war, 1938 3rd open No 4144 was photographed in September 1950.

In contrast, No 4996, a 1938 brake-composite, was seen in BR carmine and cream livery on 26 August 1948. (H.C. Casserley)

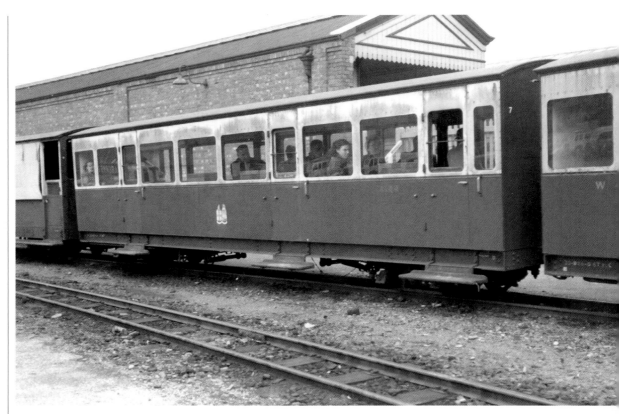

No 4144, a 3rd open liveried in carmine and cream, on an unknown date. (N.J. White)

One of the two cattle vans built by the GWR in 1923, photographed on 15 August 1935. Regauged, they were sent to the Welshpool & Llanfair Light Railway in 1937. The one sold to the Ffestiniog Railway by BR in 1960 returned to Aberystwyth in 2014 and was restored by apprentices in the new workshop in 2017.

A Plynlimon & Hafan wagon photographed on 15 August 1935.

A Plynlimon & Hafan wagon with a Midland Railway Carriage & Wagon Company wagon. The GWR replaced the wheelsets of most of the wagons during its tenure, increasing the wheelbase in some cases.

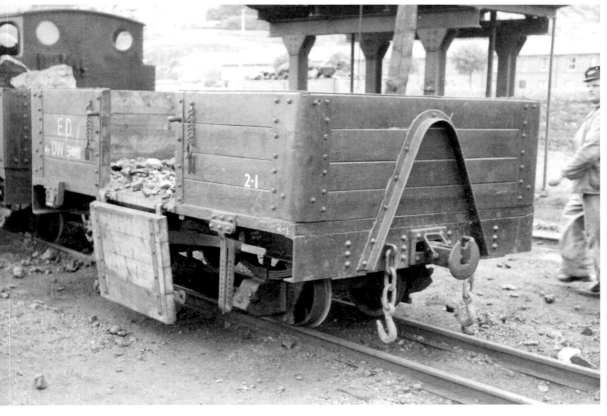

Two ex-Plynlimon & Hafan Railway wagons carrying coal, stabled on the harbour branch stub.

Midland wagon No 34111 was nominally attached to the engineers' department for ballast, but such demarcation has been ignored.

One of the Midland wagons loaded with coal in 1956.

Six wagons loaded with ash stabled in the station headshunt in 1978.

Little and large wagons at the tranship siding in 1948.

A similar scene on a different site in 1978.

An array of wagons at the tranship sidings circa 1970.

A wagon converted as a flat, a bolster wagon and a Midland wagon in the 1930s.

Originally a standard gauge machine, this Wickham trolley, a permanent way personnel carrier, was re-gauged and allocated to the railway in 1963. Seen here in 1980, it was withdrawn in 1985 and is preserved at the Apedale Valley Light Railway in Staffordshire.

CHAPTER 4

THE SUBSIDIARY YEARS

For the next 79 years, the railway was a subsidiary of a larger railway company, the local Cambrian Railways, the regional Great Western Railway and the nationalised British Railways, later British Rail, although it remained nominally independent until Parliament validated the Cambrian's acquisition in 1913.

News of the takeover was first published in the *South Wales Daily News* on 5 August 1910. Five days later John Conacher reported to the Cambrian board that 'certain directors of and other friends interested in the Cambrian company had acquired a controlling interest in the Vale of Rheidol Light Railway Company.' The Rheidol directors dealt with the transfers of shares and debentures on 26 August 1910 without comment.

Reporting the change in ownership on 11 August, the *Aberystwyth Observer* enthused about the possibilities that would follow electrification. Journey time would be halved and trains more frequent. House building along the line would be encouraged. A possible extension to Rhayader or Llanidloes would reduce the journey time to South Wales considerably. Taking a swipe at the railway companies generally, it said they 'are passing through arduous times,' forced to electrify their suburban lines by tramway competition, tramways demonstrating that carrying 60 people for 6d each was more remunerative than carrying 12 for 1s, a lesson, it said, that the GWR was slow to understand. The motor car had taken away the 1st class traveller, and railway companies were now more dependent on their 3rd class passengers. It forecast that the Rheidol valley might become more populous if electrification was carried out efficiently.

In response, surely, to the change in control, one of the remaining minor shareholders placed an advertisement in the *Welsh Gazette* (13 October) offering his shares, quantity unspecified, for sale, saying, 'This Railway has been doing very well lately and under the able directorship of David Davies, Esq., M.P., may be expected to do better.' If the railway had been doing that well it was unlikely to have come under the control of the Cambrian directors.

On the railway, Edward Davies, a platelayer, was in the wars on 23 August. He had been instructed to go from Nantyronen to Devil's Bridge, but the train, which was full, did not stop. He judged that it was going slowly enough for him to be able to jump on the footboard of the brake van as it passed, but he missed his footing and sustained severe bruising as he was dragged along 'for some distance'.

When the directors met on 5 October 1910, Pethick announced that owing to the transfer of 'certain ordinary stock' A.R. Fowler and N.F. Pethick were no longer eligible to be directors. He therefore proposed the election of Thomas Craven and John Conacher in their stead. Alfred Herbert was elected to replace C.E. Cottier at the same time, and was elected chairman on 14 March 1911.

Pethick submitted his own resignation on 6 October and was replaced by C.B.O. Clarke. Just J.W. Szlumper remained of the old regime so the Cambrian had de facto control of the railway, and not only through the Pethick assets but also the Works Syndicate shares. A few shares remained in private hands, including those of former directors.

During the autumn, in a reversal of what might have been expected, Samuel Williamson, Denniss's newly appointed successor as general manager and secretary since 1906, conducted what is now called

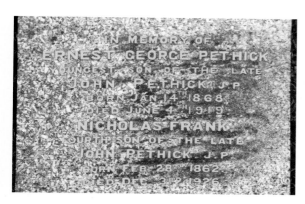

Nicholas Frank Pethick, who oversaw the railway's construction for his father and brothers, is buried in Plymouth's Efford cemetery, sharing the plot with one of his brothers, Ernest. Two other brothers, Arthur, who succeeded H.H.M. Smith as chairman, and John, are buried in the same cemetery, Arthur's grave being unmarked.

'due diligence,' enquiring further about the railway, its assets and its liabilities. His list of the 30 employees is reproduced in Appendix 7. In 2017 the railway had 37 employees, six of them engaged on administration.

The land bought from the council at Aberystwyth in 1902, and only half paid for, was one of the liabilities. No conveyance had been prepared, Williamson understood, because the railway's solicitor was also the town clerk. In 1914 the council tried to make completion conditional on the harbour branch being paved. The sale had still not been completed in 1916 because the council was unable to prove that it owned the land in the first place, and the Cambrian could, if it wanted, claim possessory title because it could demonstrate occupation since 1902. It dragged on.

For the time being there were no alterations to the railway's administration although notice to quit the London office by 25 March 1911 was received from Pethick Brothers in December; the registered office was moved to Oswestry on that date.

Notified that the Territorials were returning to Lovesgrove with 5,000 men at Whitsun, 4/5 June, Rees sought permission to reinstate the previous

year's arrangements. On receiving his assurance that the arrangements were not in contravention of Board of Trade regulations, permission was given. Perhaps the directors were right to be cautious. There had been no consultation with the Board of Trade and no expenditure on the tablet machines necessary for a loop to be properly managed.

Both rail and sleepers were replaced during 1911. Because Rees had been unable to obtain any second-hand sleepers he was given permission to buy new. He was also authorised to sell the stock of old rail, valued at £30, and to use the money to buy new rail. On the locomotive front, he was given permission for Williams & Sons, Aberystwyth, to repair *Prince of Wales* against an estimate of £50.

The link with the Cambrian had become even closer by 5 April 1911, with that company's secretary, Samuel Williamson, acting as secretary, although he was not confirmed in that position until 19 September. The accountant was given notice that his appointment would be terminated on 31 December and that he was relieved of his duties immediately. The Cambrian's audit office clerks subsequently received £5 between them for their services in preparing the half-yearly accounts.

Fresh arrangements were made for the combined rail and coach tours in 1911, with the company arranging to hire a charabanc from Commercial Car Hirers Ltd. The 20-seat vehicle cost £17 per week and was hired in August and part of September.

Some employees were given a day off with pay to celebrate the coronation of King George V on 22 June 1911. Those who had to work were allowed a paid day's leave in lieu.

John Conacher died on 18 October 1911, prompting the inclusion of a fulsome tribute in the minutes. Davies, the largest shareholder, was elected as director to replace him on 10 January 1912. Later in the year, C.D. Szlumper, the engineer, died on 27 October, aged 41, and Smith, the first chairman, on 10 November. Conacher was

John Conacher, chairman of the Cambrian Railways when its directors bought the Vale of Rheidol Railway's shares in 1910, died on 18 October 1911. He is buried in London's Highgate cemetery.

The railway's first chairman, Henry Herbert Montague Smith, died at Bourne End, Buckinghamshire, and is buried in Fenn Lane cemetery, Little Marlow.

Charles David Szlumper, the railway's resident engineer, is buried in Richmond's public cemetery. His parents were buried with him in 1914 and 1926.

buried in London's Highgate Cemetery, Szlumper in Richmond, and Smith in Little Marlow, Buckinghamshire.

Further steps to bring about the full integration of the railway with the Cambrian were taken in 1911, when on 6 December the Rheidol directors resolved that the locomotive and permanent way departments be placed in charge of the Cambrian's equivalents, with effect from 1 January 1912 for the former and at a date to be arranged for the latter.

On 14 February 1912 the directors approved the fitting of centre couplings to 15 wagons, cost £6 14s, unspecified expenditure on the harbour branch, £50 on signalling apparatus and £20 of repairs to the loco shed. The engineer was to produce an estimate for providing a carriage inspection pit. Without comment, this was the last time they met.

The demands of the tourist traffic and the territorial camps put pressures on the locomotive fleet that could not easily be met. In 1912 the Festiniog Railway was asked if it had a locomotive to spare, its directors agreeing on 20 July to provide one, adding that the daily charge should be £1 5s for the loco and driver. With modifications to its coupling gear, the England 0-4-0STT *Palmerston* spent several weeks at Aberystwyth, an arrangement that was repeated for several years.

Reporting on flooding that had resulted in passengers returning from Devil's Bridge by road on 24 August, the *Manchester Guardian* added that the temporary bridge across the river installed by the Army had been washed away.

The Cambrian directors formally resolved to take over the railway on 6 November 1912. £15,022 'A' 4% debenture stock would be issued in exchange for £16,900 Rheidol debentures and £12,715 for £51,000 ordinary stock. The amounts were calculated on the basis that the 'A' stock would reimburse the 'friends' their £23,000 investment, allowing for the stock being worth 94% of its par value and producing, at 4%, at least the same interest

as the Rheidol debentures and shares. The calculations also took into account that the debentures were also not worth face value, a move that had the effect of slightly increasing the value of the shares.

Two days later Alfred Herbert wrote briefly to the shareholders informing them of the proposed takeover, writing again in more detail on 17 December 1912, explaining that the debentures became redeemable at par on 31 December 1914 and it was considered impossible to raise this amount except on onerous terms. The railway needed additional locomotives and rolling stock and 'a considerable amount' spending on the track. The Cambrian would take over the whole of the debentures and assume all the liabilities, including £1,354 12s 5d overspent on the capital account, and pay all expenses of the amalgamation. He observed too that £24 of 4% stock would produce 27¾% more than £100 Rheidol stock had in 1910 and 1911. It was pretty much a paper exercise as the Cambrian's nominees already controlled the debentures and most of the ordinary stock.

Amongst the shareholders were four members of the Pethick family, four of the Szlumper family, Brunner,

Only one photographer is known to have photographed the Festiniog Railway's 0-4-0STT *Palmerston* during its visits to the railway. In this view at Aberystwyth station two of the carriages have been painted in the Cambrian Railways' livery. (K.A.C.R. Nunn)

Mond & Company, Cottier, Madge, Mellowes and Francis, the latter one of the original promoters. Brunner, Mond owned the Cwmystwyth mine and was later a part of ICI; the company had acquired its shares in 1909. Thirteen shareholders, not just current or former directors, held sufficient shares, £250 or more, to entitle them to be elected directors.

The Cambrian's intention to deposit a Bill for permission to take over the railway and for other purposes had been advertised in the *London Gazette* on 19 November 1912.

Evan James Evans, a chemist, was one of only two shareholders with an Aberystwyth address, and he objected to the proposals. On 26 December 1912 he wrote to Herbert saying that he spoke for 250 shares and would get his friends and others to object unless he received the face value of the shares. In his report to the Cambrian directors on 7 January 1913, Manager Williamson noted that Evans had bought his shares for £150 in 1906 and had sold 70 of them for £43 10s. Evans persisted with his objections into 1913, even getting Herbert to meet him in Aberystwyth.

Another objector was C.S. Denniss, the former Cambrian general manager, who complained that issuing more 'A' debentures to acquire the railway would reduce the 'alarmingly low' value of those already issued even more. Writing on 26 February 1913, he thought the proposal was a mistake and 'cannot be any great advantage to the Cambrian', apologising for having to 'express these divergent views'.

Williamson wrote to Rheidol shareholders and debenture holders on 1 August, explaining that under the terms of the Act that had received the royal assent on 4 July, the railway had been amalgamated into the Cambrian as from 1 July 1913. He asked for their certificates to be sent to him, to be exchanged for Cambrian 'A' debenture stock. The surrendered debentures were in the names of Davies and his two daughters, Craven, Clarke and Herbert; they also controlled £46,400 of the ordinary stock.

Wrapping up the administration of the amalgamation, the Inland Revenue required conveyance duty to be paid at 1% of the liabilities (£1,706 15s 4d) and on 87% of the debenture stock issued to the Rheidol shareholders, £12,693, and debenture holders, £15,018, total £258 10s. Loan capital duty of £34 15s was also payable.

The only time the effect on personnel was considered had been on 4 June 1913 when Williamson told the Cambrian directors that they must be prepared for the Rheidol staff asking for parity of pay and conditions with their new colleagues. It had not been the Cambrian's practice to make any distinction between personnel working on the main line and the branches and light railways but in this case he thought that any attempt to change pay and conditions should be resisted.

The question that must be asked is, why after rejecting Pethick Brothers' overtures since 1906, did the Cambrian finally agree to take on the railway? Was it simply that the vendors had become so keen to sell, being prepared to accept a lower price that made sense in terms of investment potential? – a mistaken belief that it was a bargain, despite the engineer forecasting a substantial sleeper renewal programme at an early date and replacement of the loco and carriage sheds. The onset of the Great War prevented the Cambrian from having to spend too much money on it, however. The sheds never were replaced.

From this point there is less information to be found about the railway from official records. The most notable change to the railway under Cambrian control was to the locomotives. They had their names removed and were repainted. Nos 1 and 2 were sent to Oswestry works, where they had their bunkers enlarged, increasing the locos' width by 12in and the handbrake layout altered. It was also decreed that a jack should be carried on the front running plate, for use following derailments.

A report on the state of the railway and to determine where savings could be made was submitted by the Cambrian's senior officers, W.H. Williams (traffic), A. Craig

The Cambrian Railways removed the locomotives' names and the original company's crests, as seen in this view of No 2 at Devil's Bridge.

No 1 at Devil's Bridge in 1921, after it had visited Oswestry works and returned with a new paint scheme and enlarged bunkers. (W.L. Good)

Another view of No 1 at Devil's Bridge in its Cambrian Railways condition.

Born in Dolgellau, John Pryce Morris joined the Cambrian Railways as a cleaner in 1886, was promoted to fireman in 1887 and driver in 1896, although he gave his occupation as 'railway engine stoker' in the 1901 census. His employment record states that his record was poor and that he was confined to branch line duties. He left voluntarily in August 1901 and joined the Vale of Rheidol Railway on 7 July 1904, so the Cambrian got him back. A poor eye test in 1928 restricted him to the railway and to shunting duties. He retired in 1932, due to 'trade depression', received a pension of 15s per week and died on 3 November 1943.

(loco department) and James Williamson (permanent way) on 3 November 1913. Rees had been consulted.

Since 1 October one engine had worked the service except on Wednesdays and Saturdays when an extra train required a second loco. From 1 November the entire service could be worked by one loco, but the hours of duty required two crews. By rearranging the duties and running the last return trip with a Cambrian driver and fitter's assistant Millman, a passed fireman, the services of a fireman, £1 4s per week, could be saved. The loco crews did not sign on or off duty. The service should be worked by *Rheidol* as it used less coal although it was under repair. Trains comprised one carriage only except on market days and early closing days.

Joiner W.J. Jones was shared between the loco and permanent way departments. He was no longer required by the former but sharing his services on carriage and wagon repairs with 'the Cambrian proper' would save the expense of sending someone from Oswestry.

Traffic personnel were station masters at Aberystwyth, Capel Bangor, Aberffrwd and Devil's Bridge. At Aberystwyth there was a guard and a 'transhipper'. A 'summer hand' covered for holidays until 6 November. None of the others could be spared. The decrease in ore output meant that the transhipper, B. Goulding, would not be fully occupied but the transhipping charge of 3d per ton on coal, lime and merchandise covered his wages; casual labour would be difficult to provide and would cost as much. Goulding could clean carriages or help with station duties if not engaged on tranship work. Guards cleaned the carriages, when time allowed, at the terminals.

Rees could take on the position of Aberystwyth canvasser as well as having oversight of the railway. As canvasser he would look after the area from Carmarthen to Glandyfi; this would entail trying to poach GWR traffic from the former Manchester & Milford Railway. He could also look after the Cambrian's interests in

Aberystwyth, which the joint station staff could not do.

Switching out the loops at Capel Bangor and Aberffrwd during the winter or working the railway by staff-and-ticket was considered. At the latter, the 'boy's' wages would be saved but the cost of disconnecting the loop and providing a new set of instruments would exceed the saving. Notice that the traffic department's station master is now a boy. Capel Bangor could be switched out but the volume of goods traffic would still require the 'man in charge' and ticket issues by the guard would delay the trains. Staff-and-ticket working received little consideration in view of the heavy summer traffic. New locking equipment would be required at the exchange sidings, Nantyronen, Rhiwfron and Capel Bangor and there would only be a benefit if station personnel could be withdrawn.

The Cambrian's 1913 working instructions give an insight into train operating:

- Sounding three long whistles at milepost 9½ warned the Rheidol Mining Company that the train had goods to be unloaded at Rhiwfron.
- Tickets were checked and collected at Aberffrwd (up trains) and Llanbadarn. Carriage doors were locked on the station side after tickets had been collected at Llanbadarn. Ticket checking on up trains had been transferred to Capel Bangor by 1919.
- Timber and other traffic carried on two or more wagons was not attached to passenger or mixed trains.
- Traffic on the harbour branch had to be accompanied by a guard who warned 'trespassers' of the movement; loco crews were to exercise the greatest vigilance and caution.

Rees claimed, in 1943, that timetable changes did a lot of damage to the railway. First the early-morning trains were

dropped, then the equivalent evening trains, leaving only a skeleton service. The withdrawn trains would have carried only a small amount of local traffic and probably did not pay, even if *Rheidol* was used to haul them.

To deal with the anticipated extra traffic accompanying the annual Territorials' camp, on 26 February 1914 the traffic department was given permission to arrange for the hire of a loco from the Festiniog Railway on the basis of paying £25 for two weeks in August plus £2 per day over 14.

As the Rheidol river bank at Aberystwyth was suffering from scour and the nearest property was the railway, the council thought, on 28 April 1914, that the Cambrian should make a substantial contribution towards the £800 estimated cost of repairing it. The Cambrian's engineer objected, pointing out that the wall between the railway and the river predated the railway and belonged to the council; if the damage continued, the wall, which acted as a flood defence and protected a large area of the lower part of the town, would be damaged before the

railway. It was to protect the town that the remedial works were required, not just to help the railway. With the Cambrian probably the largest rate payer in the area affected, he could not recommend making a contribution unless all the landowners contributed.

The council was persistent, putting pressure on Davies, now the Cambrian's chairman, and a site meeting took place. Of all the property likely to be affected by flooding only the railway was not council owned. If the Cambrian did not contribute to the repairs the council would do nothing, expecting that the Cambrian's works to protect its own property would also benefit the community. This was undoubtedly a bluff, stated the engineer in December 1914, but if the council did allow the wall to be damaged the railway would have to tip stone along the river bank. 144 tons of stone from Devil's Bridge was donated to the council in lieu of a cash contribution. On 16 April 1915 the *Cambrian News* reported the council's public works committee's decision to defer the work as it had been unable to obtain any contribution from the railway.

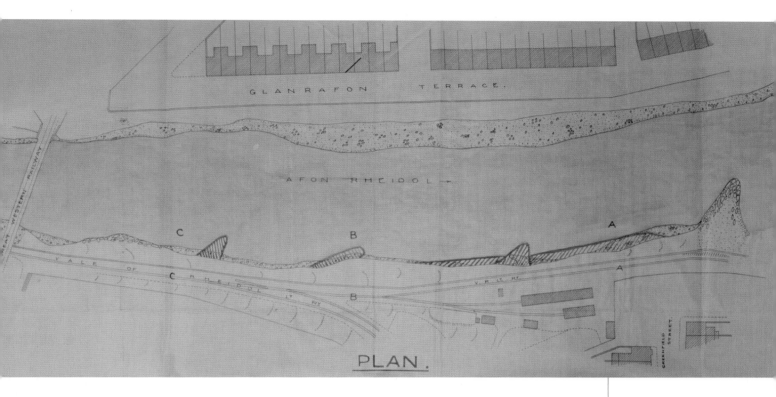

PLAN.

After an inspection, another report, unsigned, was submitted on 18 October 1914. No tail lamps were carried on the trains. Rule books and appendix were to be sent to each member of staff. At Devil's Bridge the record keeping of parcels arriving was poor and Hafod Arms Hotel staff took parcels while the station master was busy, avoiding the administration. Calves were carried but there was no rate for them. There was no list of cloakroom charges and the station master did not realise that bicycles and packages left on the station should be charged for. The station master said that he should not be blamed as he had not been properly instructed.

At Aberffrwd and Capel Bangor the waiting sheds would be improved by a cement floor, there were no parcels rate books, and the tablet registers were not fully kept up. At the time of the inspection there were only two vehicles in the Capel Bangor carriage shed. A common complaint for all stations was the delivery of parcels without a signature being obtained.

This report leaves the impression that the Cambrian made little effort to integrate the railway and then wondered why its procedures were not being observed. Rees was no doubt busy with his canvassing duties and there appears to have been no one individual with responsibility for the railway. Transferred to Oswestry in June 1916, Rees retired from railway service in 1932 and was aged 81 when he died at Bow Street in 1953. He is buried in the churchyard at Llangorwen.

The railway was not directly affected by the war until March 1917, when the Cambrian wanted to release the station master at Capel Bangor. It decided to suspend tablet working and to work with 'one engine in steam' instead, providing the Board of Trade with a sealed undertaking dated 4 April. Tablet working was to be resumed in April 1919 although the sealed undertaking was not made until 5 May. In October 1920 the Cambrian suspended the railway's tablet working for the winter months as an economy measure. Realising that this would be a regular feature of operating in the future, the newly created Ministry of Transport suggested modifying the undertaking to avoid it being renewed twice a year.

This plan of the proposed flood defences on the Afon Rheidol at Aberystwyth also shows the track layout of the area around the loco shed. (National Archives)

A measure of the impact that managing the railway had on James Rees can be had by the knowledge that more than 30 years after he had ceased to manage it his position as manager was recorded on his grave at All Saints, Llangorwen.

AND
IN LOVING
MEMORY OF
JAMES REES, BRYNMELYN,
FORMERLY MANAGER VALE OF
RHEIDOL RAILWAY, WHO DIED
24 Nov. 1953, AGED 81 YEARS.
AND WHEN EVEN WAS COME HE
PASSED OVER TO THE OTHER SIDE

The Cwm Rheidol mines had changed hands in 1918, the new owner asking for the Rhiwfron siding to be replaced. He offered to pay £20 for the work and to complete the standard agreement for its use.

Two burglaries in 1917 were linked although only the first concerned the railway. The mother's situation and the magistrate's comments are also a reminder of the social conditions of the time.

Aberystwyth station had been broken into on 22 July, and David John Evans and Owain Glyndwr Evans (both aged 8), cousins, appeared in court a few days later charged with having stolen 7s 6d worth of chocolate which they had eaten in a carriage. Station master A.E. Humphreys gave evidence that £2 2s 3d of tickets were missing too. When Elizabeth Evans, David John's mother, said that she was out in service, that she had five children, the youngest seven months old, that her husband was in the navy and that she could not manage on the £1 13s 6d weekly allowance she received, and that her sister-in-law and her four children were visiting to allow her to work, the magistrate, the town's mayor, lectured her that she should have stayed at home or left the children in a place of worship. The mothers

This portrait of the Devil's Bridge station building is dated October 1916. The wagon sheet visible on the left of the photograph is branded with the railway's name, not that of the Cambrian Railways. The building was listed Grade II by Cadw, the Welsh heritage agency, in 1989.

were ordered to pay the cost of the chocolate and the boys were birched.

There was a follow up in September when St Peter's church was burgled, and Owain Glyndwr Evans and his younger brother Maldwyn appeared in court. Nothing had been stolen but evidence was given that Owain had committed thefts before, and his mother said that although he had been birched for the Vale of Rheidol station theft, 'the real offender was afterwards found'. Their father was serving in Salonika. In this case the bench was lenient, binding the boys over for good behaviour on £10 security.

A row developed among councillors in February 1918 when the council discovered that the station land had still not been paid for. Interest on the outstanding balance (£400) had been paid until 1912 and now the council had lost sight of the transaction. A conveyance had been made in November 1917 but only £400 had been transferred to the council's account, leaving the balance, £400, plus £110 7s 8d interest, outstanding. A settlement was reached and the council invested the £800 in 5% war stock.

In April 1918, work started on felling larch for use as timber props above the Rheidol mine, the *Cambrian News* (3 May 1918) reporting that the men carrying out the work travelled to Rhiwfron on the train and walked to the work site. In October the cableway, which had fallen out of use, was recommissioned and used to carry the timber across the valley and thence by train. A hundred and twenty tons had been carried by 11 October and another 80 tons in February 1918. Presumably there were unreported shipments too.

Other timber was cut near the railway, between Rheidol Falls and Rhiwfron, disrupting traffic on several occasions when cut timber and debris fell on the line and no effort made to remove it. Following several letters and promises to protect the railway, the Cambrian eventually sought an injunction on 24 January 1919, when judgment was given for £125 damages and costs, £100 of the damages not to be claimed if the contractors replaced and repaired damaged fences to the company's satisfaction.

Despite her court appearance in 1909, Mary Edwards did not desist from walking along the railway between Rheidol Cottage and Llanbadarn. On 28 November 1918, she and her mother were both fined 5s for trespass earlier in the month. Driver John Price Morris said that he had whistled twice when he saw them, but they took no notice, forcing him to slow down. In defence they said that they had a right to walk along the line 'as everyone else did so', in which case they must have been singularly unlucky to have been caught.

The frustration engendered by the out-of-season wartime train service prompted one resident to put pen to paper with a letter published in the *Cambrian News* on 15 November, reproduced in full: 'The patience and good humour of residents of the Rheidol Valley have been put to a severe trial of late. For some years, the passenger service on the railway has been going from bad to worse. This month the trains have dwindled almost to vanishing point. If the present policy is carried further the line might as well be closed altogether. It is fully realised that all good patriots should grin and bear a great deal; but in this district we are made to put up with more than our fair share and feel that it is time to protest.

Yours, etc., Cardi'

The Retail Coal Prices Order of 1917 allowed local authorities to set the maximum price of coal. As the schedule was drawn up in consultation with coal merchants it was presumably to deter profiteering. In an order made on 12 August 1919 the Aberystwyth Rural District Council decreed that coal sold at Capel Bangor and Devil's Bridge stations could be charged for at an additional 1s 6d and 2s 9d per ton respectively.

Meeting in Lampeter on 21 October 1919, members of the Cardiganshire Farmers' Union complained about difficulties in obtaining suitable wagons for livestock. Although the secretary had already raised the issue with the Cambrian, they decided to extend their complaint to the Ministry of Transport.

An article about the railway published in the June 1921 issue of *Railway Magazine* gave an insight into the railway just before it was absorbed, with the Cambrian, into the GWR. The Bagnall 2-4-0T No 3 acted as spare to the 2-6-2Ts during the Summer. During the winter months, when traffic was light, it was usually the only engine in service, hauling trains of one or two carriages and a van.

The only change since the Cambrian had taken over was to liveries, black for the locomotives and bronze green for the carriages. No 2 had just returned from Oswestry, where it had had its footplate widened by 12in; the author did not explain that this change was to increase the bunker capacity. All the stock retained its original numbers.

Originally, the author said, No 1 was painted yellow, No 2 was medium green and No 3 was light green. The passenger stock had green underframes and the bodies were grained and varnished.

Another insight into the railway arose from the investigation of the Light Railways' Investigation Committee in 1921. This was designed to inform the government about the health, or otherwise, of light railways and whether they should be included in the forthcoming grouping of railway companies.

The Cambrian's response to a questionnaire revealed that the railway still had control of the goods traffic at Devil's Bridge because road competition existed only between Aberystwyth and Aberffrwd. Tabulated data is reproduced in Appendix 8 while other items from the return include:

- The harbour branch was unused.
- Maximum passenger train length was seven carriages, the average was two in winter, five in summer.
- Mixed trains comprised two carriages, a brake van and four wagons.

When it discovered that the river bank at Aberystwyth was still at risk of scour in December 1921, the council again asked the Cambrian for a contribution towards the repairs. The engineer was in favour of providing support but suitable stone was no longer available from Devil's Bridge and it would be cheaper for the council to buy it than the company, he reported. The outcome was not recorded.

From 27 March 1922 the Cambrian, and the railway with it, was amalgamated with the Great Western Railway in accordance with the requirements of the 1921 Railways Act. This was a consequence of the government's management, some would say mismanagement, of the railways during the First World War, where they had been effectively nationalised. During the period of government control the railways had not only been run down but there was no mechanism set in place for the companies to be compensated adequately. The grouping of railways into four regional companies enabled the larger companies to absorb and, in effect, cross-subsidise the smaller companies and protect them from bankruptcy. Compulsory fare increases in 1917, intended to discourage discretionary travelling to make rolling stock available for use on the continent, opened up the market for military-surplus motor vehicles driven by trained ex-soldiers to be put into use to carry both goods and passengers.

On 19 September 1922, 20 years after the railway had been opened, Aberystwyth town council's worst nightmare came true. After two days of heavy rain, the river burst its banks above the town and flood water raced down the railway. In no time at all, the station was flooded and then the nearby streets. The water was deep enough to need boats to rescue residents; the council's wall on the river bank was breached to relieve the pressure. After two days the water had drained from the town, but parts of the railway were still flooded. The *Manchester Guardian* (21 September 1922) expected that the railway would not be reopened for several

days and said that a motor-charabanc service had been substituted.

Any traffic records created under GWR ownership have not survived. Although the minutes of the locomotive and traffic committees record the major decisions taken, the whereabouts of the briefing notes that would have been produced to support them are unknown.

As a part of the GWR however, the railway was to benefit from more investment than at any time since it had been built, and not just on a one-off basis either. As early as 11 January 1923, the locomotive committee resolved that 'under circumstances represented by the chief mechanical engineer it was agreed to recommend an expenditure of £5,000 in the construction of two locomotives, 2-6-2T types, weighing 25 tons each for use on the Vale of Rheidol branch.' On 12 April 1923 it followed this by approving the construction of four additional 32ft open passenger cars at a cost of £2,400.

The original locomotives had been renumbered by the GWR, No 1212 and 1213 for the Davies & Metcalfe engines and No 1198 for the Bagnall. The last

probably never carried its new number, was condemned on 26 July 1924, and was cut up at Swindon. It did, however, incur repairs that cost £97 12s 4d before it was withdrawn.

No 1212 was twice sent to Swindon, firstly in December 1922, for repairs that cost £847 2s 8d, including £260 19s 3d for boiler work. It had only done 1,959 miles since its previous repair at Oswestry. Then in November 1924, having worked 15,298 miles, it was sent again for repairs that cost £334 6s 3d and which took until 25 May to complete. On this occasion the boiler work only cost £2 5s 4d. It kept its original cylinders and valve gear and received new tanks and a copper safety valve bonnet. Back at Aberystwyth it was, it is said, retained as a spare engine until it was condemned in December 1932. There is only one photograph known of it in service in this condition but several exist of it at Swindon where it was stored pending a possible sale before being scrapped on 9 March 1935.

The new locomotives, Nos 7 and 8, were delivered in October 1923, effectively versions of the Davies & Metcalfe machines adapted to

No 8, the second of the 2-6-2Ts built in 1923, powers past the flood defence wall near the loco shed soon after it had entered service. Passengers were never able to enjoy a view of the river from the train because the wall, intended to protect Aberystwyth from flooding, was not demolished until after the track had been diverted in 1968. The wall pre-dated the railway but when the floods had come in 1922 they entered the town from further upstream, as J.W. Szlumper had predicted in 1903.

C.C. Green, the author and historian, claimed that this photograph was used by the GWR to justify the construction of new Vale of Rheidol stock. Whatever its purpose, it is distinctive in being the only image known to the author of No 2 with its No 1213 plates before it was sent off to Swindon to be rebuilt and return a completely different locomotive. No other images are known of the wagon conversions with roofs attached either. Despite the fading perspective, the photograph also shows the differences between the semi-open conversions, especially as they have been arranged, from the rear, in order of conversion.

So far, this is the only known photograph of No 1 *Edward VII* rebuilt by the GWR as No 1212 in service to come to light. (N. Shepherd)

No 1212 at Swindon waiting for the purchaser who never came. It was scrapped in 1935. (C.L. Turner)

Swindon's interpretation of the Davies & Metcalfe design on shed. It looks as though the photographer has persuaded No 8's crew to pull No 7 out of the shed for him. It will be seen that No 7 had no tank-side handrails. (John Scott Morgan collection)

suit Swindon practices. They had Walschaerts valve gear, copper-capped chimneys and safety valve bonnets and were equipped with steam heating. They were three tons heavier than the Davies & Metcalfe locos and Green (see bibliography) states that they could haul trains of nine carriages and a brake van without losing time.

Now it appears that the locomotive committee then practiced a measure of deception on the accountants. In November 1923 No 1213 was sent to Swindon for an overhaul. Its record card shows that the work

The third of the Swindon locos, No 1213, in 1926. Its tank-side handrails are of a different pattern to those attached to No 8. The broken spectacle probably arose when the fireman was breaking up the coal. One of the 1923-built summer cars is stabled on the harbour branch. Funding for the water tank had been approved on 26 February 1925. (A.W. Croughton)

was completed on 24 July 1924, incurring work valued at £2,589 18s 5d, which included a new boiler, wheelsets and cylinders. Surprisingly, the work had cost almost the same as Nos 7 and 8 had cost to build from scratch. It was returned to Aberystwyth identical to Nos 7 and 8 in every significant respect, including the valve gear and cylinders; it was a new loco.

Engineers familiar with these locos have told the author that No 1213, No 9 from March 1949 until 2016, is the same as Nos 7 and 8 and could not have been rebuilt from No 1213. Green gives more details about the way the new locomotive was built without approval, but it has not been possible to track down all of his sources. It can be stated, however, that Nos 7 and 8 were funded from the capital account, whereas No 1213 was funded by the maintenance budget, from revenue.

The GWR called the four new carriages summer cars; they were open above the

waistline and could seat 48 passengers. Two cattle vans were supplied in 1923, presumably the consequence of the Farmers' Union's efforts in 1919. In 1937 they were regauged and sent to the Welshpool & Llanfair Light Railway.

Along the line, the engineers' department approved the expenditure of £2,000 for ballasting and making up cesses on 24 February 1924. Locomotive water supplies were the responsibility of the locomotive committee which, on 27 March 1924, authorised the erection of a second-hand water tank and stand pipe in place of the existing water tanks, 'in bad condition', at Devil's Bridge, the work to cost the locomotive department £255 and the signals department £10. Two water cranes with swing jibs, £125, were approved for Aberffrwd on 18 December 1924 and the installation of a larger water tank at Aberystwyth on 26 February 1925, £292.

No 7 nears the end of another journey. The second and third vehicles are summer cars, from the 1923 and 1938 batches respectively. (D.J. Davies)

A view looking eastwards just before Devil's Bridge, with the permanent way gang active on the track. (J. Salmon)

DEVIL'S BRIDGE, ABERYSTWYTH. 10057.

A shed scene in May 1939. The sheds never received much maintenance and were observed to have holes in their roofs as early as 1906. Running repairs were carried out in the right-hand building. They lasted, with even more holes, until the line was diverted in 1968.

The railway's value came in for some comment at a hearing of the Railway Rates Tribunal on 30 May 1924. Established by article 20 of the Railways Act 1921, the tribunal was holding hearings to determine the standard revenue of each of the amalgamated railway companies. It had been noticed that the railway's 1902 capital value of £69,000 had declined to £27,000 when the Cambrian had acquired it in 1913. When the National Association of Railway Traveller's barrister asked if it was right that fares should be based on the original value rather than the depreciated value, the GWR's accountant assured him that the railway would soon become remunerative under GWR management, justifying the higher value.

In 1923 the GWR had started a two-year project to rebuild the standard gauge Aberystwyth station. As the works approached completion, on 25 June 1925 the traffic committee sanctioned an extension of the narrow gauge line 'from present terminus to a site adjoining the general station now in course of construction'. The budget was £850 from the engineering department and £100 from the signal engineer. A similar scheme had been considered by the independent company in 1909.

A notice dated 16 July 1925 advised of the application to the Ministry of Transport for an order to be made under the terms of article 16 of the 1921 Railways Act. This little-used device allowed railway companies to make minor alterations, extensions or improvements to existing facilities provided that the cost did not exceed £100,000, avoiding the need for an expensive Act of Parliament. In this case the extension could also have been achieved by means of a Light Railway Order.

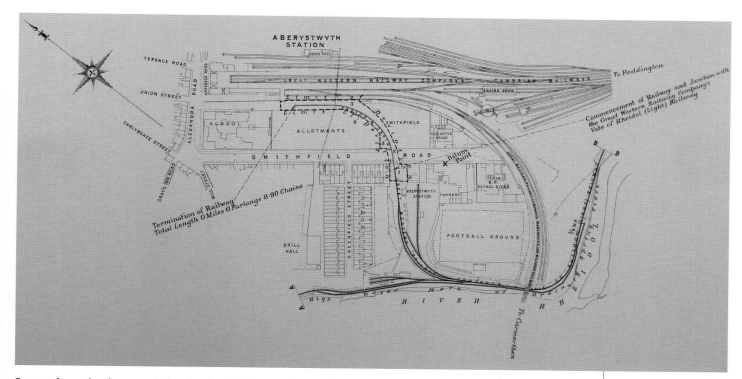

Extract from the deposited plan for the 1925 extension at Aberystwyth. (Parliamentary Archives)

Seen from the street, the end of the line for the 1926 station.

The level crossing to the new station. (Adrian Gray collection)

The order was made on 20 October 1925. It authorised both the extension, 'commencing by a junction with the Vale of Rheidol (Light) Railway of the company at its termination and terminating at a point in the road abutting on the western side of the Aberystwyth station of the company's Cambrian Railways six chains or thereabouts south-east of the junction of that road with Alexandra Road' and the acquisition of the necessary land from the town council. The capital works ledgers contain details of the expenditure. (Appendix 8)

Opened without comment in 1926, the extension appears to have been overlooked when the remainder of the Aberystwyth works were inspected. In future, passengers would get their tickets from the main booking hall and there would be no need for separate station staff.

The money spent on these capital projects indicates that the GWR thought that the railway was worth supporting,

although there must have been some concerns about costs for it was one of 53 branch lines subject to a review completed in March 1926. The results for 1924 and 1925 were tabulated but a full comparison was not provided. In 1925, 3,959 tons of minerals, 540 tons of merchandise and 32 trucks of livestock had been carried. The last item gives the lie to the claim that there was no livestock traffic to be had on the railway. (Appendix 10)

No explanation was given for the increase in staffing costs over the two years but had they remained at the 1924 level then in 1925 the railway would have made a profit. The report recommended annual economies of £1,527 by dispensing with the station master at Devil's Bridge, reducing services to single-shift, eight-hour, operation and reducing winter services to Mondays and Saturdays only. The timetables show that the last was not put into effect. Comments on a meeting

No 8 crossing Smithfield Road before the road surface had been reinstated. (Adrian Gray collection)

No 8 running round in the new station. The shed on the left appears to have been used as a waiting room. The small one on the right was used by the permanent way gang. (H.B. Tours)

Nos 8 and 1213 prepare to leave on 26 August 1948. (H.C. Casserley)

A mixed train at Rheidol Falls in the 1920s. (Francis Frith)

77697. ABERYSTWYTH, RHEIDOL VALLEY.

held to discuss the report on 30 June 1926 cast some doubts on its methodology so probably little notice was taken of it. The report however did recommend the abolition of 1st class travel from all branch lines and that measure was adopted from September 1926.

Sir James Weeks Szlumper, the engineer involved in the promotion of three schemes for railways to Devil's Bridge, died at his home in Kew Gardens on 26 October 1926 and was buried in the public cemetery at Richmond.

On 27 November 1930, the traffic committee acted on the railway's costs, resolving to withdraw the goods service from 1 January 1931. It also decided to suspend the passenger service during the winter months, using road motor services in lieu of both. The passenger services on the Corris and the Mawddwy Railways were withdrawn from the same date. The services were unremunerative, the *Times* (13 December 1930) had been told, and adequate compensatory road services, whether for passenger, parcels, or goods traffic, would be provided in each case by the Crosville Motor Services and the Western Transport Company.

More expenditure was approved by the locomotive committee on 28 October 1937. The original carriage stock had been condemned, prompting a decision to spend £7,995 to replace it. The estimates were produced in such a way as to produce an element of betterment, the difference between what the vehicles 'should' cost and what they 'would' cost. The traffic committee agreed to pay the £681 difference, the remainder being allocated to the renewals account. The stock was itemised as follows:

The reason for this working is unknown but the placing of a wagon between the loco and a brake van is most unusual. The train is also running wrong-line at Aberffrwd. (John Scott Morgan)

To be condemned			To be built		
Description	No of vehicles	Estimated replacement cost	Description	No of vehicles	Estimated cost
Thirds	10	£5,659	Thirds	10	£5,900
Brake thirds	2	£1,142	Brake thirds	2	£1,240
Brake vans	3	£513	Brake vans	3	£855
	15	£7,314		15	£7,995

No 8 with a well-loaded train circa 1930. The brake van is hidden by the locomotive's bulk. (John Scott Morgan collection)

An article in the *Great Western Railway Magazine* (July 1938) stated that the 56-seat thirds and 48-seat brake thirds were bogie carriages built on steel underframes with oak and teak body framing and internal cladding of birch. Like the 1923 stock, it was 32ft long, 6ft wide with steel clad exteriors. The brake vans were four-wheeled, 13ft long and 6ft wide. Three of the thirds were summer cars. The old stock was scrapped; according to Green, some parts were reused.

It would be interesting to know the logic behind the ordering of both the brake thirds and the brake vans. Perhaps those responsible were unaware that the goods service was no longer operating. Nevertheless, the investment, at a crucial time in the railway's, and the world's, history secured the railway's future by providing it with equipment that would stand outside in all weathers without maintenance for five years.

On the outbreak of war in September 1939 services were withdrawn without comment. Four open carriages were stored in the Capel Bangor shed, the remainder outdoors at Aberystwyth, as they always were.

With the return of peace, a service of two trains daily was operated from 23 July 1945 according to the *Welsh Gazette* on 26 July but the 'restoration of passenger services on the Vale of Rheidol branch' was not formally approved until the traffic committee met on 28 March 1946. The paper said that the train had comprised six carriages and a van, and that 80 passengers had travelled, that the driver was John Edward Davies, the fireman was Roger James, and the guard was J.E. Trevor. District inspector Evans also travelled, and the train was seen off by the station master, Herbert Roberts, inspector T.H. Trevethick and detective inspector Idris John. Davies had joined the railway as a fireman on 21 December 1902, aged 15.

Along with the remainder of the GWR, the railway became a part of the nationalised British Railways' Western Region on 1 January 1948, placed under the command of the divisional traffic manager at Cardiff.

According to Green, No 7 was repainted in GWR livery in 1948, ensuring that the initials of its former owner plied the Rheidol valley until the end of the

A busy day at Devil's Bridge on 15 August 1935, for the traffic has brought all three locos to the station. A rake of wagons is visible beyond the goods shed and a part of one of the cattle vans peeks into the picture on the left. The carriages and the visible loco still have their steam heating equipment. (H.F. Wheeller)

No 1213 is thought to be the only loco to have had the GWR's 'shirt-button' logo applied. On the left is a glimpse of one of the 1938 carriages.

A GWR train takes water at Aberffrwd in 1948.

Still in its GWR livery, No 7 climbs up to Nantyronen, with a train of carmine and cream carriages in 1953. Troedrhiwfelen is just visible through the trees.

1953 season. It would make more sense if such a perverse act had been carried out in 1947. Nos 7 and 8 were sent to Swindon in April 1954, which was probably when they were both painted green, with the first BR logo applied to the tanksides. No 1213

was painted black and renumbered No 9 in March 1949.

The earliest item surviving in the BR-era files is dated 8 April 1953 and dealt with what became a common theme of the railway's post-war years – would it be

An unusual angle on No 7 in Swindon works in 1954. (John Scott Morgan Collection)

Twelve months after its visit to Swindon, No 7 stands at Aberystwyth waiting for passengers to arrive.

Three locomotives in the same livery lined up in numerical order after they had been named, 26 June 1956. No 9 (formerly No 1213) has had its smokebox number plate removed while carrying an 89C (Machynlleth) shed plate. It still retains the connector to its steam heating gear.

reopened and would it be available for sale or lease? In this case the enquirer was a G.C.W. Beazley, a Bedfordshire farmer, and the answer was that there were no plans to close the line and arrangements were being made 'for the usual operation of passenger trains this summer.' On 31 August Beazley wrote again that he had heard rumours that the line was to be closed and expressed his willingness to take it over; again he was told that there were no plans to sell it.

The date that LMS-style numberplates were fixed to the locomotives' smokebox doors is unknown, the earliest dated photographs being taken in 1953. The existence of photographs showing the mounting brackets and no numberplate in 1957 or later may be a record of a driver expressing a personal preference.

Over the three years from 1955 the locos ran in three different liveries. In 1955 Nos 7 and 8 were plain green while No 9 was black, all had the first BR logos affixed centrally to the tanksides. In 1956 they were all plain green and were named, with the crests moved downwards to accommodate brass GWR-style nameplates. In 1957 they were repainted green and lined out in full GWR fashion with transfers of the second BR logo mounted under the nameplates.

Publicity with the operation of evening excursions and the resumption of Sunday services in 1955 attracted increased numbers, and led to the locos being named and the carriages being painted GWR chocolate and cream from post-war lake and cream at the same time. The decision to turn out the trains in full GWR style may not be unrelated to the visit made by BR's western area board in the spring of 1956.

Another boost for the railway occurred on 24-26 July 1957 when the Royal Welsh Show was held at Llanbadarn. With echoes of the pre-First World War camps, eight-car shuttles ran to the showground with a loco at each end. According to a local newspaper, trains ran at 12-minute intervals, achievable, according to Green, by moving the Aberystwyth tablet machine to the showground site and declaring it to be within Aberystwyth station limits. 25,260 return tickets at 6d were issued, many more travelled only one way, and the railway maintained its normal service to Devil's Bridge.

Great changes occurred during the 1960s, socially and on the railways. The advent of budget holidays at exotic destinations where the sun could be guaranteed to shine, and the increased use of cars, had an

effect on both the traditional British seaside holiday and the railways. The development of preserved railways that had started in Wales in 1951 had shown that there was a market for steam railways, even in the face of modernisation that was to see steam removed from the national network. Preservation had demonstrated that with the input of enthusiasm and volunteers steam railways could attract passengers and pay their way, but they needed to be regarded as entertainment rather than as a pure means of transport.

With regard to this railway, BR was always going to struggle to find a balance. On the one hand, the unions would always insist that the driver of a train to Devil's Bridge was paid the same as the driver of an express to King's Cross. On the other, it had all the resources one could ask for to ensure that maintenance and repairs were carried out quickly and effectively and, with a bit of imagination, at marginal cost. It is clear that many of the managers involved with it over the years were either enthusiasts or enthusiasts for it,

who wanted it to be successful and to be a part of the national network.

Mounting losses incurred by the railways under the management of the British Transport Commission (BTC) increasingly concerned the government. The situation was partly self-inflicted; costs, particularly wages, were rising but the government would not allow fares to be increased. Dr Richard Beeching was appointed chairman of the British Railways Board (BRB) from 1 June 1961 with the objective of reducing costs. BRB took over from the BTC on 1 January 1963.

With services restricted to the summer, the railway would not have figured in the network-wide traffic survey conducted for Beeching in April 1962. However, when the divisional managers were consulted about lines that might be closed it was not overlooked. At a divisional conference held on 21 August 1962 it was agreed to sell it as a going concern.

The managers were informed by a correspondence between the divisional traffic manager and traffic headquarters

Seen crossing Smithfield Road in the 1960s, this view of No 7 demonstrates that there was little effort put into cleaning the locos at this time. During the 1950s the loco had received a pair of tank-side handrails like No 8's. (Mervyn Mason)

Moving the locos backwards and forwards between Aberystwyth and Swindon for heavy maintenance would have done nothing to help reduce the railway's costs, the movements apparently calling for special trains and the steam crane. Here No 9 was returned on 20 April 1960 and No 7 has arrived at Plascrug to take it to the shed after it has been unloaded. The ballast train comprises three Plynlimon and three Midland wagons, two flats loaded with sleepers and two bolster wagons.

at Paddington under the heading of 'unremunerative railway services – Aberystwyth–Devil's Bridge' that had been started in January 1962. The cause was the 'estimated deficiency of revenue' of £2,340 in 1961 and the overdue decision on whether the railway should be run during the forthcoming summer. In 1961 28,387 passengers had earned £6,818; the adult return fare for the full journey had been 6s. This compared with 31,395 passengers earning £4,570 in 1960 when the adult fare had been 3s 6d. No explanation was given for the large increase; the size of it implies that the results for 1960 had been marginal.

The traffic costing officer produced a report dated 24 January and the costs for 1961 are shown in Appendix 11. When trains were running, a ganger, sub ganger and two length men were employed full time, although it had not been possible to determine where the costs of three ballast trains run during 1961 had been allocated, he added. Although additional summer season signalling posts had been authorised, in 1961 the district relief men had been used.

Closing the railway would not result in immediate savings. The costs included

provision for interest and renewal of locos and rolling stock. Labour costs related to men employed elsewhere and who would not be laid off if it closed. Costs would be affected (increased) by the introduction of a 42-hour week.

Sending the report on to London, the divisional traffic manager asked for approval to operate the line in 1962 and said that he would review the position in the autumn, analysing train loadings and the use of personnel. Permission to operate was given on 5 February 1962, with a rider that the 6s fare, 3d per mile, was the maximum allowed by statute and could not be increased.

On 5 September 1962 the Western Region's accountant wrote that although 1961's working expenses had actually been £12,590, increasing the deficit to £5,770, they included interest and depreciation on the rolling stock, £4,149, and non-variable overheads of £1,241 which should be disregarded. As a result, the deficit was only £380 'which is not significant'. He pointed out that the deficit was almost equal to the cost of publicity.

R.F. Hanks, the chairman of the BTC's Western Area Board, had written to the

No 8 at Swindon, stripped down to facilitate removal of its boiler. (Cutting Edge Images)

region's general manager on 28 August 1962: 'I fear the days of the … very attractive little railway are numbered.' Observing that societies had been formed to purchase 'old and out-moded' railways', citing the Talyllyn and Festiniog Railways, and saying 'neither of these had anything like the attractive assets we can offer in the case of the Vale of Rheidol Railway … by dint of a good deal of enthusiasm and hard work by volunteers they are running again', he suggested that the railway should be valued and advertised for sale. 'We might get much more this way than by merely closing it, pulling up the track and having left on our hands the locomotives, rolling stock etc.'

Approval to sell the railway was given by the BTC on 6 September 1962, with a rider that the commission's operating powers could only be transferred to a new owner by means of a light railway order.

The decision to sell the railway was addressed on 19 October, the various departments being asked to submit valuations of the line and its equipment on 6 November 1962. Receipts for the year were £6,368 from 26,849 passengers. 147 passengers per train generating £34 8s 9d in 1962 compared with 137 passengers and receipts of £32 13s 2d the year before because the number of operating days had been fewer. Costs, reduced to £10,950 largely because of a reduction in civil engineering expenses, produced a deficit of £4,580.

The valuation was produced on 14 December 1962, in time for a meeting with members of Aberystwyth town council on 17 December. The rolling stock valuation was scrap value, its gross replacement value being £63,990 (Appendices 13/14).

The meeting took place at Paddington. The railway made a small profit without taking renewals into account, but when major capital expenditure was required it was inevitable that it would be recommended for closure. No case could be made for hardship that the Transport Users' Consultative Committee could use to recommend retention. The line had been valued at £140,000, an amount that was too high to be considered, therefore, on the basis that by reducing wages and staffing levels the railway could make a profit of £1,500 to £2,000. The council could buy it for £20,000. Or, to put it another way, an investment of £20,000 might earn up to 10%. These figures were pure guesswork, for the railway team had no idea what wages the council would have to pay or how many employees it would need.

When the council team tried to negotiate on the price, they were told that it was not negotiable. It was subject to survey however, and the council had three months to respond. From 1 January 1963 it would have to negotiate with the London Midland Region (LMR) which would then be taking over responsibility for the former GWR lines in mid-Wales. The details were confirmed by the town clerk the next day, when he concluded by stating that the council's preference was for the railway to be continued under BTC control.

On 7 January 1963 the LMR informed the town clerk that the survey had revealed minimal liabilities over the next five years – permanent way, £770; bridges, £400; fencing, £20; painting, £90.

News of the offer to sell the railway started to leak out. The National Trust declared an interest and after a story about the possible sale had been published in the *Cambrian News,* Beazley wrote again, too. The council failed to respond to a letter seeking information about its intentions on 3 April, leading to the LMR writing, 'I presume that your council is no longer interested …' on 26 April 1963.

The town clerk replied straight away. Yes, the council was still interested but as it had heard that arrangements were being made for trains to be run it had assumed that it had been withdrawn from sale. This was a rather fatuous response. Arrangements had been made to run the line because the council had been quiet on the subject since the meeting the previous December and it had ignored the letter of 3 April.

The 26 April letter was mistimed, for unknown to Euston a meeting with council representatives and the divisional manager at Chester had taken place at Aberystwyth on 25 April 1963. The outcome was that the LMR decided to make an effort to promote the railway during 1963 with a target of attracting 5,000 more passengers and turning the loss into a profit. If it did not succeed, then the railway would be closed. The council played its part by accepting that it had a responsibility to create fresh business for the railway if it was to continue in BR management.

The effort was worthwhile. By 25 August, 27,122 passengers had earned £6,135 compared with 21,913 earning £5,159 over the same 12-week period in 1962. At the end of the season a profit of £610 was declared. This had been aided by the unremarked-upon removal of the loops at Capel Bangor and Aberffrwd; the railway was now a much more basic railway. During the year a Wickham trolley was allocated to the line to aid permanent way maintenance. The Capel Bangor carriage shed was probably demolished at the same time the loop was removed; it had survived into BR days only with the aid of poles supporting its walls.

An irregularity concerning the goods service was uncovered in March 1964, for although it had been withdrawn by the GWR in 1931, the stations were still listed as freight depots. After due processing, the stations were listed as only handling passenger and parcel traffic from 1 June 1964.

On the stock, the LMR made its mark by painting the carriages a dark green, intended to represent Cambrian bronze green, lettered VofR on the sides in gold, in 1964. It did not wear well and apparently some were repainted, without the lettering, within three years.

Another would-be purchaser surfaced in August 1965, when Roland F. White of Cromar White Developments Ltd,

miniature railway engineers, declared an interest. He was told that, while it was true that the railway's circumstances were reviewed occasionally, no firm decision as to its future had been taken.

The 1965 review reported income of £10,820, including £900 attributed to other stations and £300 of miscellaneous income from Devil's Bridge; there were no through bookings, the £900 was an estimate of re-bookings. Costs of £9,040 comprised £5,990 for movements (operating), £400 terminal and £2,650 for track and signalling. There had been two drivers, two firemen, a guard and two signalmen, one each at Aberystwyth and Devil's Bridge,

all posts for the summer only. There was no allocation of personnel for permanent way or other maintenance. The ordinary return was still 6s but there were also cheap day returns of 4s in the off-season and 5s in the peak season. These compared with the 6s 1d return bus fare, a situation that attracted the suggestion that they should be increased.

In 1966 a loss of £2,128 was made. The Stoke-on-Trent divisional manager, George Dow, who now had responsibility for the railway, was asked to report on the situation and did so on 11 April 1967. The principal reason for the loss, he explained, was the limited use that could be made of train

Stabled near Devil's Bridge, the permanent way gang's Wickham trolley in September 1967, soon after it had been delivered to the railway. It had been built in 1947 as a standard gauge machine. (Cutting Edge Images)

New liveries were introduced in 1957, Western Region passenger livery for the locos and the not-much-liked 'Cambrian' green for the carriages, the combination seen here with No 9 in charge of a heavy (seven carriages) train. (David Mitchell)

Whenever the uphill water column at Aberffrwd failed, up trains ran into the loop to take water from the downhill column. The fireman grapples with the valve on 26 May 1965. (Cutting Edge Images)

On 29 May 1957, the facing point lock failed at the Devil's Bridge station throat, with catastrophic results for the train, although fortunately there were no injuries. (John Field)

crews outside the holiday season. At the present time they were used to relieve staff undergoing diesel training but that was not a permanent solution. He would like to investigate the possibility of employing medically-fit retired railwaymen on a seasonal basis; doing so would save £3,217 a year although he realised that the unions might not agree to it.

Savings might also be achieved by straightening the line at Aberystwyth, a move that would eliminate a level crossing and produce a plot of land that could be sold to offset the cost. It would also allow the standard gauge locomotive shed to be used as 'much improved garaging accommodation' for the railway's rolling stock.

These changes would make the line viable in the short term, but expenses were still likely to increase and the time would come when no more economies could be made. Dow proposed a two-stage programme. Firstly, to make the line profitable and, if possible, to divorce its operation from BR by using seasonal staff; then to seek a council guarantee to cover any future revenue shortfall. If the council would not agree then the possibility of a sale would have to be investigated.

The report did not refer to a meeting that had been held on 3 March 1967, where it had been agreed to develop a scheme to divert the railway into the main line station and to make the standard gauge locomotive shed, closed in April 1965, available to it.

Dow was instructed not to open negotiations with the unions over staffing as doing so might only give short-term relief and could be abortive, but that the time was right for a sale to be pursued, especially as the locomotives and rolling stock would not incur heavy maintenance costs for 'a year or two'. As it would take time to conclude a sale and it was desired to sell the railway as a going concern, he should proceed with plans to operate the 1967 season.

Writing to the LMR's assistant general manager on 19 May, Dow thought that his recommendations had been dismissed in a cavalier manner. Surely the land requirements should be clarified before the line was offered for sale? He had written after attending a 'priorities meeting' on the same date, where the general manager had given verbal approval to realigning the track. Its £2,800 notional cost would release land valued at £7,000-8,000.

By the time that a reply was sent to Dow on 1 June 1967, the British Railways Board had approved the line being put up for sale. The question of the realignment and the disposal of the surplus land could be dealt with as a part of the disposal, the purchaser might want to buy the land as well. The assistant general manager agreed with Dow that BR's staffing agreements were inappropriate, saying that the effort involved in changing them was out of proportion to any possible gain.

A letter from Dow to the general manager dated 26 June 1967 explained that the seasonal signalling post at Devil's Bridge was normally covered by an Aberystwyth-based relief signalman but in 1966 it was covered by a redundant guard.

Dealing with a maximum of four trains a day at that time, this would not have been the busiest post on BR. In another letter on the same date, he mentioned that one of the reasons that the line did not cover its costs was because it paid the trainmen for 52 weeks while it only needed them for 16 weeks. He was instructed to inform the staff and the council that consideration was being given to selling the line.

The railway's profile was raised considerably by a visit from the minister of transport, Barbara Castle MP, on 1 July. En route to a Welsh Labour rally at Aberystwyth, she joined a train at Devil's Bridge. Asked about the line's future, she said that BRB had made no proposal to close it. While this was true it paid

No 8 in its Western Region livery on Llanbadarn level crossing on 8 August 1964. The tower of St Padarn's church, built on the site of an earlier structure in 1257, is visible over the cab. The loco has been given No 9-style tank-side handrails. (KR Photographics)

no regard to the situation or the fact of a sale not being a precursor to closure. The ministry had been briefed in advance of the journey and Dow had briefed the minister during it. Following newspaper reports about the proposed sale and a display of anger by the council, the minister's Parliamentary secretary demanded an explanation.

The key to what was called a 'misunderstanding' was that the ministry failed to understand the subtlety of the statement 'there is no proposal to close the line, but the position is reviewed at the end of each season'. BR admitted that while the LMR had not informed the ministry of its intention to sell the railway, the final decision on a sale would be the minister's, who would have to decide whether or not to make a light railway order.

BR officers met at Aberystwyth to consider the railway's position on 13 July 1967. The standard gauge level crossing at Llanbadarn, 80 yards from the railway's crossing on the same road, was due to be automated. A suggestion that the railway might be realigned to run parallel with and adjacent to the main line to eliminate its crossing was rejected because of the amount of agricultural land that would be required and the peak summer service was only three return trains a day.

At Aberystwyth, two options were considered for realigning the track. Retaining the existing station site was considered impracticable owing to the existence of the cattle market on some of the land that would be required for the altered route. The alternative was to use the Manchester & Milford Railway bay on the south side of the station. This would have the advantage of bringing the railway close to the standard gauge locomotive shed and save BR the expense of demolishing it.

Dow was informed on 19 July that the area board had agreed to sale as an alternative to closure. He was still expecting the council to buy it although he thought the Western Region's price of £20,000 was far too low. Within a few days political pressure had both changed and

clarified BR's position. On 24 July Elystan Morgan, the MP for Cardigan, posted a written Parliamentary question calling upon the minister to use her powers to prevent the line from being sold. Three days later, he too was told that the minister would be the final arbiter for any sale.

It will come as no surprise that by 2 August 1967 BRB had decided to 'disengage' from negotiations with the council on the basis that it intended to continue running the railway itself 'a bit longer'. Despite all the publicity and talk of closure at the height of the season, the railway still made a loss of £954.

During the summer arrangements had been made to relocate the terminus into the former Manchester & Milford Railway platform, disused since 1964. Before it could take place the Shell Mex & BP oil depot, served by a private siding on the stub of the Carmarthen line, required removing to the goods yard. As BR's programme left the oil company with insufficient time to relocate its installation a temporary pipeline was required. The works order for the alterations was issued on 21 February 1968.

Work on the realignment was well underway but arrangements for using the loco shed still had not been finalised. On 25 April 1968 the general manager wrote that he was prepared to agree to its use providing that it was only used for storage, that any servicing and repairs were carried out outside, otherwise the building would be regulated by the Factories Act. As no one would be working in it for more than 21 hours per week the Offices, Shops & Railway Premises Act would not apply either. The existing inspection pit in the shed must be filled in too; he was emphatic about that.

As the figures (Appendices 15/16) show, the works were not carried out to budget and were not finished on time. The additional work was carried out in December 1969/January 1970 after experience had revealed shortcomings in the original scheme. There was no complaint about the overspend, perhaps because the

By climbing into the coal wagon, the photographer has gained enough height to put the loco shed area in context with the river, the harbour branch stub, the connection with the main line and the Manchester & Milford Railway Bridge. The last placed a restriction on the height of the railway's rolling stock until the route was altered. The railway route along the river is now a footpath, the shed site a car park. (Cutting Edge Images)

7½ acres of land released by the realignment was valued at £26,625. When the works order was closed in December 1970 the total expenditure was given as £7,489 including the pipeline, an underspend of £1,740. The cost of removing the platform canopy in 1968/9 was probably absorbed into the station maintenance budget.

At Easter, 13-16 April 1968, the last trains ran over the old line and on Monday, 20 May the first train over the new line, the 14.15, was waved off by the mayor-elect of Aberystwyth, Ceri Jones. Intriguingly there was, as shown in Appendix 16, a cost of £75 to accommodate passenger trains at the former Cambrian exchange siding 'during first week', probably the Easter operation; the significance of this has not been uncovered.

The point of diversion between the original line into Aberystwyth, to the left, and the 1968 line, laid as far as the footpath in this early 1968 view. (David Mitchell)

At Easter 1968 the last trains to run out of the GWR's 1926 station were also the first to run in the new blue livery. (David Mitchell)

The end of the line in the Carmarthen bay platforms in 1968. Any thoughts that passengers might have had that they would be sheltered by the canopies were soon shown to be unfounded when they were demolished at the end of the year.

Approval to keep the internal pit was given on 18 June 1968, after the chief mechanical and electrical engineer had complained. A 'fairly extensive' overhaul of locomotives and carriages had been carried out during the mild winter of 1967/8 with great difficulty, there was a considerable backlog of essential maintenance required on the locomotives due to neglect over a long period. The nature of the work justified main workshop repairs but with conscientious and cooperative staff and experienced supervision it could be carried out at Aberystwyth provided facilities were reasonable. The heavy maintenance had to be done during the winter and covered accommodation was essential to avoid delay due to weather and lack of light.

To comply with the Factories Act expenditure in the order of £1,655 was required. Before approval was given, Dow was told 'An amount of £3,740 has already been invested in this unprofitable line … I would like to know what adaptation of the pit is likely to cost.' The estimate was £150 but it actually cost £350.

Services in 1968 were accompanied by the introduction of mechanised ticket issuing. At Aberystwyth the five most common tickets were issued using an Ultimatic machine while other issues were made from a Setright machine. Guards were also issued with one of these for issues at intermediate stations and Devil's Bridge.

Accompanying this modernisation, the signalling at Devil's Bridge was removed, permitting the signalman's post to be abolished, and the distinction between the arrival and departure lines ceased. Train control by staff and ticket was introduced, minimal signalling at Aberystwyth protected any local movements when a train was on the main line. At Devil's Bridge train crews would use the telephone to obtain permission from Aberystwyth signal box to depart. The ticket machines cost £251 and the staff savings were £450. The guards were paid an extra £44, in total, to compensate them for the extra work entailed in issuing tickets at Devil's Bridge as well as the intermediate

stations. An estimated £100 car park revenue would be lost at Devil's Bridge, the implication being that the signalman had supervised the car park, issued tickets and looked after the trains. Why the changes to train operating were linked to the ticket issue mechanisation is not clear.

Corporate 'rail blue' livery was also adopted in 1968, the double arrow symbol being applied in white. The work had been carried out at Aberystwyth and was seen for the first time at Easter, 13-16 April. Along the line, all the stations and halts received new signs in the standard format, white with black lettering.

So, with its new station, new livery, new tickets and new signs, the railway of 1968 looked very different from that of 1967. Dow retired on 29 June 1968 – he should have been well satisfied with what he had achieved, except that he had no legal authority to make the diversion, which would cause BR's solicitors some head-scratching 20 years later.

An undated and unsigned consultant's report on the railway appears to have been compiled during 1968. Correspondence in another file suggests that it was compiled by John Crawley, an enthusiast better known for his interest in road steam vehicles, and submitted, with an apology for delay, in July 1969. The adoption of the rail blue livery deprived the railway of its character and was an error of judgment, he wrote. The new layout at Aberystwyth was an operational improvement but hid the railway from public view; previously the terminus was alongside the largest car park and coach park in the town. At Devil's Bridge the station was tucked away, the signing was poor. The timetable left a lot to be desired and was sparse.

Recommendations included painting the locomotives and carriages in GWR livery, erecting 'steam railway' signs at the termini, establishing a shop in a portable building at Devil's Bridge to replace the existing outlet in the old weighbridge office, locating two Pullman cars at Devil's Bridge as a catering facility, retaining

The east end of the loco shed in 1978, showing the coal tranship siding and the rail bolster wagons.

card tickets, introducing a railway letter service, running inclusive DMU excursions complete with refreshments, improving the timetable and reinstating Aberffrwd loop.

The report concluded that the railway was ripe for exploitation. Although efforts had been made, having a manager who could run the line and exploit it would be better. 'I would also imagine that the railway suffers at the hands of the BR accountants in arriving at charges for work done by the different departments. Given a fair chance the railway could be made profitable, the extent of which will depend upon … the funds … put aside … for future maintenance.' Some of the recommendations were acted upon, the timetable was improved, without a loop, Devil's Bridge got catering but not Pullmans, a shop was set up in the station building, a railway letter service was started in 1970 and signage was improved.

After 15 September 1968 the railway was the only steam service operated by BR. 48,532 passengers carried during the year earned £12,873 but the deficit was £15,000.

The future of the railway between Aberystwyth and Machynlleth was threatened by the possible sale of the railway to a 'London-based syndicate', the Aberystwyth Trades Council and the Association of Locomotive Engineers & Firemen, declared in February 1969. In 1967 only 31,000 passengers had left the town by the main line train compared with 47,000 who had travelled to Devil's Bridge by steam train. A two-year grant to support the line to Shrewsbury, which had been under threat of closure, had been announced a few days before but they felt that its future was still insecure and would be weakened if the railway's traffic was lost. They also objected to the round-trip fare being increased from 7s 6d to 10s.

The syndicate had first approached BR to enquire about the possibility of buying the railway in February 1968. Despite the uproar after the minister's visit the year before, BR was still a willing vendor and, notwithstanding the minister's antipathy towards the idea, BR had engaged with the ministry to establish a strategy for its disposal. Rather than formally closing the line before disposing of it, it should be sold as a going concern to the highest bidder who was able to obtain a light railway order. The price had been reviewed and bids in the range of £20,000 to £27,000 would be sought. On 11 July 1968, John Bernard Snell, the syndicate's spokesman, told BR that he wanted to complete the sale by around 1 January 1969.

Snell was an enthusiast, who in the 1970s became the general manager of the Romney, Hythe & Dymchurch Railway. Many years later he was quite rude when he told the author about aspects of the railway's operation that he had seen, that he was certain that its efficiency and viability could be improved.

The minister was moved to a new post in April 1968, removing one possible obstacle to a sale, although her successor Richard Marsh's approval to it had not been obtained. The political pressure was continued though, in the form of a letter from John Morris, MP for Aberavon, who had holidayed at Aberystwyth and found himself bombarded (probably an overstatement) about the railway's future.

Correspondence with Snell continued throughout 1968. Nothing could be done until the minister sanctioned a sale, he was told. He asked for the surplus turnouts from the old terminus to be retained for sale with the railway and was concerned to see the entire redundant track listed for sale by the stores department in October. He was told that although the sale could be deferred for a short time, deterioration caused by much delay would reduce its value – perhaps he should make an offer for it. The invitation was declined: 'we are not interested in becoming small-scale scrap merchants.' With the sale of the land to the council proceeding, the track was lifted and put into store alongside the loco shed before the year's end.

Although the correspondence was ultimately fruitless, Snell was treated seriously by the LMR's assistant general manager, I.M. Campbell. In November 1968 he submitted a copy of a business plan and draft of a letter to be sent to the council for comment. On 25 November he pointed out that the railway's omission from the list of unremunerative lines to be subsidised or likely to be subsidised made it difficult to avoid speculation about its future. He had asked the enthusiast press to avoid commenting on the railway but would not do so again. Campbell, however, did not take kindly to Snell's proposal that a notice should be issued about the negotiations, saying that the correspondence had been conducted on a personal basis and that Snell had not been negotiating with BR.

Eventually the minister was persuaded to take a position on the railway's future, telling Campbell, then the LMR's general manager, on 7 May 1969 that he had decided 'not to proceed with the sale of this line in the near future.' 'In the near future,' Campbell was told, was code for 'not before the next general election'. Would-be purchasers and others concerned should be told that this was the board's decision and that it would be better to say 'during the next two years' in preference to 'in the near future'. Snell was informed of the decision by letter dated 12 May.

His response must have been unexpected. So far as he was concerned the situation was unchanged. The decision was obviously politically induced, the Shrewsbury–Aberystwyth line's subsidy expired at the end of 1970 so therefore BR intended to operate the railway during 1970. The syndicate's involvement was founded on the basis that it was correct for BR to dispose of the railway and that BR agreed that it was a policy to be adopted when circumstances allowed. A company would be formed, and he would be in touch.

The Vale of Rheidol Railway Limited was registered on 12 August 1969. Its objectives were to purchase or otherwise acquire 'the railway now existing between Aberystwyth and Devil's Bridge … and to carry on the business of running a railway.' With Snell, the shareholders were Geoffrey Stuart Drury, John Brian Hollingsworth, Patrick Bruce Whitehouse, Patrick John Garland, Peter Christopher Allen and Richard Hugh Dunn. They were railway enthusiasts of the first magnitude.

Drury and Hollingsworth owned standard gauge steam locomotives. Snell, Garland and Whitehouse had been involved in the revival of the Talyllyn Railway, and Garland and Whitehouse had strong links with what are now called the Birmingham Locomotive Works, Tyseley, and the South Devon Railway. Allen was the chairman of ICI, the major chemical company, and of the Transport Trust. Dunn was a solicitor with strong links to the Severn Valley Railway.

Snell informed BR and the council that the company had been formed but only told the latter the company's name. On 27 August 1969 the council's town clerk wrote to BR: 'The use of this name … must assist in giving the impression … that the company has a proprietary interest in the railway …' Was BR aware of the intention to form the company and did it object to, or propose to object to, the use of the name, he asked?

Apologising for not having told BR about the name, Snell said that it was an oversight. Internally, BR's solicitor wrote that he doubted that the company's name was 'so misleading as to be likely to cause harm to the public,' the only cause for objection after a company has been registered, but he was willing to make representations if required.

Letters of complaint about the company were sent to BR by the rail unions, resulting in BR having to defend its position to the local MP and Campbell formally terminating his correspondence with Snell. Campbell informed the council that little would be gained by objecting to the company name. However, the council's response and the other letters prompted a change of view, 'that it might be politic' to make a formal protest to the registrar of companies.

Before protesting, BR's solicitor decided to see if the company could be persuaded to change its name voluntarily. As a gesture of support, the name Vale of Rheidol Equipment Limited was chosen, BR was informed on 10 November 1969.

In 1969 the railway made a profit of £229 on a turnover of £20,073 and carriage of 50,000 passengers. Takings at the new Devil's Bridge shop, which sold souvenirs and refreshments, were £1,580 from stock purchased for £1,370; it had not been open for the full season. A longer season and operation of more trains in 1970 resulted in 118,000 passenger journeys being recorded, up from 69,000 the year before (*The Times* 18 January 1971). Passenger journeys record return tickets as two journeys, enabling comparisons to be made with other attractions. BR's in-house catering operator, Travellers Fare, took over responsibility for Devil's Bridge catering in 1978.

Dialogue between Snell and BR was resumed in 1970, apparently at the latter's instigation (the copy of the letter concerned is missing), although the relationship soured in November when Snell revealed that the company's name had not been changed. He argued that as the company was inactive there hadn't seemed much point. There is nothing more in the BR files relating to it.

The company bought two 0-8-0s from the recently-closed Mecklenburg-Pommersche Spurbahn for possible use in 1970 and 1972. The second, which had a tender, was inspected by BR engineers while it was in store at the Ffestiniog Railway but failed to see how it could be usefully adapted for the railway. Both locomotives were sold in 1978 and the company was struck off the register of companies in 1984.

With the objective of promoting the railway under BR ownership, the Vale of Rheidol Railway Supporters' Association was established in 1970, run from the district manager's office at Stoke-on-Trent. Members received a quarterly duplicated newsletter and a discount voucher for travel on the railway. *The Guardian* (14 March 1970) reported that 140 enthusiasts joined within two weeks.

There had been changes in BR management, and the government elected in June 1970 might have brought with it a change in policy regarding the railway. At the end of the year the LMR asked the divisional manager at Stoke to make a financial case for sale or retention. Results for 1970 were much better: turnover of £29,233 producing a profit of £4,951, including £800 from the shop.

The divisional manager reported on 24 March 1971. If the line was to be sold, he recommended starting at £150,000 and being prepared to settle for £100,000. The realisable assets, locomotives, carriages and track were worth much more than the £30-40,000 previously proposed as an asking price.

While the headquarters' files concentrate on the railway's financial position, there were developments on the ground that escaped attention. In December 1970 No 7 was sent to Chester wagon repair shops for a light overhaul and No 9 was sent there for a general overhaul 12 months later; this was not the first time that one of the locos had been sent other than to Swindon, for No 9 had been sent to Oswestry in the 1960s.

To increase capacity, the Devil's Bridge siding was extended to permit the station to accommodate three trains simultaneously for the 1972 season. The 38-yard extension cost £345. The extra trains were expected to increase revenue by £800.

Reorganisation within BR in 1974 saw responsibility for maintenance taken over by the area maintenance engineer at Wolverhampton and for operating by the area manager at Shrewsbury. The latter was previously dealt with from Machynlleth.

In 1974 No 7 was sent away again, this time to Swindon, where it received a new

No 7 receiving attention at the former Cambrian Railways' Oswestry works in the early 1960s.

Three trains at Devil's Bridge in 1972. The siding had been extended by 38 yards to make this possible. (E.T.W. Dennis)

No 7 at Aberffrwd in 1975. The loco has been lined out but the carriages are still in 1968's plain blue.

boiler. It was returned to traffic in June 1976. Its blue livery had been enhanced by being lined out in black and white, brass BR logos being applied to its cabsides. In September 1975 three carriages and the brake van were sent to Shrewsbury station where Wolverhampton-based personnel carried out repairs in a workshop established on an unused platform. They too were repainted with the BR blue livery lined out in black and white. One carriage was repainted in this form at Aberystwyth. All were in traffic by June 1976. Further carriage overhauls were carried out at Chester. The overhaul No 9 received at Swindon in 1976/7 reportedly cost £25,000 (*Birmingham Daily Post* 7 April 1977).

Facilities at Devil's Bridge also received attention in 1974. A portable building accommodated a new ladies' toilet and a connection was made to the mains water supply. The space previously occupied by the ladies was incorporated into the shop. The budget was £1,900.

The hot summer of 1976 increased the risk of lineside fires, which was mitigated but not eliminated by cancelling the morning trains during August; an estimated 25,000 passenger journeys were lost. As a result it was decided to convert the locos from coal to oil firing, adopting the system already in use on the Ffestiniog Railway. No 7 was converted first and trialled in February 1978; the equipment required was made at the FR's Boston Lodge works. Using ordinary diesel fuel, 150-gallon tanks had enough capacity to work two round trips, 50 gallons per journey going uphill and 20 gallons downhill. A storage tank was installed alongside the loco shed at Aberystwyth and the exchange siding at the east end of the loco shed was removed. In September 1977 No 8 was sent to Swindon and two carriages and a van to Shrewsbury. The locomotive work, which included repainting in the same style as No 7, cost £75,000.

A landslip on the site of the Alltddu workings, near the Erwtomau mine, 10 miles from Aberystwyth, closed the line from 6 July 1979, when a part of the embankment slipped into an

A van and one of the 1923 opens seen at Shrewsbury in 1975. A workshop was established on the otherwise unused platform to repair and repaint Rheidol stock, the black and white lining being applied at the same time.

No 9 shunting through the east end of the loco shed in 1981.

When the locos were converted to oil firing a standard gauge tanker wagon was obtained in which to store the oil.

old mineshaft. The mine had been worked from below the railway, leaving a 40ft x 5ft wide 'chimney' some 240ft deep, emerging close to where the toe of the railway embankment had been built. A rail-and-sleeper cap was constructed to seal the 'chimney' and the railway reopened after four days. The mine is recorded as being worked in the 1850s and was probably abandoned when the railway was built.

Changes to liveries were started in April 1981, when No 8 appeared in GWR green, complete with shirt-button logo, the repainting carried out at Aberystwyth. The divisional manager explained that the new livery was part of an effort to revitalise the railway. It started a trend, and sponsorship was

obtained for more repaints. When No 9 was turned out in 1902-style livery in 1982, the work was sponsored by Richard Metcalfe, a descendent of James Metcalfe, not knowing that the locomotive had been built by the GWR in 1924. Shell (UK) sponsored the repainting of No 7 in Western Region livery in 1983 and in 1986 No 8 was repainted again, being turned out in Cambrian Railways livery, lettered Cambrian and with its nameplates removed. Gala events that accompanied the launch of the new liveries attracted large crowds.

The carriages were not ignored either. From 1982 transfers of the original crest were affixed to the bodysides, then from 1983 the fleet was repainted in GWR livery, a paint company sponsoring the

The last steam-hauled works train, May 1988. Delivery of the diesel locomotive was expected within a few weeks. (Andrew Bannister)

Before No 8 appeared in Cambrian livery on 5 May 1986, it ran for a short period in this intermediate scheme. (Peter Heath)

No 9 in its faux 1902 livery crosses the river bridge in 1983. The first carriage is the vista car, No 4999, designed to give its passengers the best of the views but lacking ventilation and much heavier than the other vehicles. It was out of service by 1989.

work. Also in 1983, the Wales Tourist Board and the Development Board for Rural Wales sponsored the conversion of one of the carriages into a vista car, travel in the vehicle attracting a supplement. In 1983 and 1984 the Westinghouse Brake & Signal Company Limited sponsored the conversion of the brake/3rds to brake/1sts. In 1986 two of the carriages were named *Myfanwy*, after Myfanwy Talog, a TV announcer, and *Lowri*, for Laura Ashley, the Carno-based designer.

A series of special trains and events through the 1970s and '80s helped to keep the railway in the public eye. No 9 spent a few weeks on display at the National Railway Museum over the winter of 1982/3 but the highlight was the visit of the Ffestiniog Railway's Alco 2-6-2T *Mountaineer* on 13/14 September

1986. Despite this effort, the traffic figures inexorably declined and by 1987 they were less than they had been in 1969.

Notwithstanding the declining revenue, a Permaquip personnel carrier had been supplied to the line in 1985, replacing the Wickham trolley. In 1986 a fibre-glass liner was fitted in the GWR water tank at Aberystwyth, and in 1988 Mid Wales Development made a grant of £15,000 towards the £45,000 cost of a 140hp diesel locomotive, the first to work on the railway. A diesel hydraulic machine in 0-6-0 configuration, it was built by the Brecon Mountain Railway using components made by Baguley in Burton-on-Trent for an export order that had been cancelled. Normally used on works trains it can be used on passenger trains in an emergency.

No 9 celebrating the railway's 80th anniversary at the National Railway Museum in January 1983.

The Ffestiniog Railway's Alco 2-6-2T *Mountaineer* seen in action during its visit in September 1986. (Hugh Ballantyne)

The Permaquip personnel carrier crossing the road at Llanbadarn in 2018.

The new diesel locomotive on test on 24 May 1988. Two of the carriages are in the throes of being repainted. (Andrew Bannister)

Whatever profits were made by the railway, they were insufficient to cover the costs of renewals. A derailment at Nantyronen on 26 May 1986, where two carriages turned on their sides, demonstrated that underneath the fresh paint the railway was not as sound as it should have been. The loss in 1986 had been £108,000, and with a Conservative government in power since 1979 thoughts were turning to privatisation of the railways. More than ever there was no reason for BR to be involved in the operation of a tourist steam railway.

The derailment had, incidentally, occurred just a few days after a train hauled by No 9 was involved in a collision with a lorry on the level crossing at Llanbadarn, where traffic levels had increased since the road had been incorporated into what was effectively the town bypass. The crossing was automated in 1989.

Work on evaluating the railway's future started early in July 1987 and a report was submitted on 27 July. The options were: to retain the line in BR ownership and restore it to profitability; make an agreement with Ceredigion District Council whereby BR would operate the line and the council would promote it and cover losses; outright sale. If the line was retained a loop would be reinstated to increase train frequency and operating flexibility. If it was sold, a price of at least £250,000, the current valuation, should be sought. (Appendix 18)

A group of employees decided that they would like to acquire and operate the railway and in May a friend, a former railwayman, had approached the Conservative Party suggesting that the railway could be disposed of to them at a nominal price with an announcement timed to coincide with the June election. A letter confirming an earlier telephone call being passed to the Department of Transport, the minister, David Mitchell MP, replied that it was for BR to decide on the railway's future and that he had forwarded the letter to BR's chairman, 'asking him to consider your proposal'.

On 27 August 1987 the group informed board members of its plans, pointing out

Seen in 1991, the railway's second Wickham trolley was this 1976 machine transferred from the Brecon Mountain Railway in 1989.

that if it bought the line it would recruit from the existing pool at Aberystwyth, avoiding transfer/redundancy costs 'or legislative difficulties' and would promote share ownership amongst the staff and increase through traffic from BR.

The board agreed the steps to be taken to sell the railway on 14 September 1987. In summary, the sale would comprise these elements:

- Register a company
- Make a scheme under Section 7 of the 1968 Transport Act to transfer the assets to the company
- Issue tender documents inviting bidders to tender to buy 100% of the company's share capital
- Initiate closure procedure once a successful bidder had been chosen and paid 10% deposit
- When consent for closure had been given, the vesting day for the asset

transfer would be set, the successful bidder paying the balance of the purchase price within a specified period of time

On 16 September J.K. Welsby, BRB's managing director of procurement and special projects, told the Department of Transport the rationale for selling the railway. Its geographical remoteness and unique nature made it difficult to manage effectively. Considerable management time would be required to make the changes required in manning and versatility to reduce staff costs to reasonable levels. The best option was to sell the railway.

The ministry saw 'no problem in principle' to the sale, asking that any announcement should make it clear that it was subject to the secretary of state's consent, that the line was a unique part of BR, being narrow gauge, and only used for part of the year.

BR's legal advice was that it could not sell the railway without formally withdrawing the service, so it was necessary to withdraw the service only when a buyer had been identified. Lazard Brothers & Company were appointed to handle the sale based on being paid a retainer of £20,000 per month from October 1987, plus a success fee of £60,000 and expenses.

A press release announcing the intention to offer the line for sale was issued on 18 November 1987. Not unsurprisingly this attracted some media interest. Under the headline 'BR severs its last link with the age of steam', *The Daily Telegraph* (21 November 1987) reported the line had an estimated value of more than £1 million, that four potential bidders had already expressed an interest and that two scrap merchants had been told that their offers would not be considered.

The employees, now a consortium of eight employees plus five friends, had reiterated their interest in taking over the railway on 7 October. By cancelling the bidding process and selling to them for a nominal sum BR would save on the fees charged by the bank appointed to handle the sale, they wrote. The sale would not take place within the present parliament without 'our active blessing and co-operation'; the closure procedure and the weight of public opinion ensured that.

BR obtained an off-the-shelf company named Crodall Limited on 4 November 1987, the date it had been incorporated, and renamed it Vale of Rheidol Railway Limited on 24 December. £100 share capital was created and on 5 August 1988 £1 was issued to Britravel Nominees Ltd and £1 to the British Railways Board.

BRB's chief accountant had unexpected difficulty producing figures relevant to the railway, writing to colleagues on 7 January 1988 that he had discovered that its cost centre had been used as a 'dumping pot' for miscellaneous headquarters expenditure, instructing that more care be taken to ensure that the figures were accurate.

From BR's perspective, the Department of Transport upset the applecart in a letter sent to its solicitor on 24 February 1988. Although the 1968 Transport Act could be used to transfer property rights and liabilities it could not be used to transfer operating rights. Therefore a light railway transfer order would be required. There was considerable debate about the rights and wrongs of this approach but in the end both procedures were followed.

It was determined that whatever happened, 1988 would be the last year BR would operate the railway – the timetable leaflet even bore a black flash with the legend 'last year in British Rail ownership'. Following the publication of advertisements soliciting interest in the railway in January 1988, the invitation to tender, a 44-page brochure, was issued on 6 June and the advance notice of BR's intention to close the line was published on 29 June.

Seeing a draft of the information memorandum that accompanied the brochure in May, the railway inspectorate's Major Peter M. Olver had said that the

The tender document issued by Lazard Brothers in June 1988.

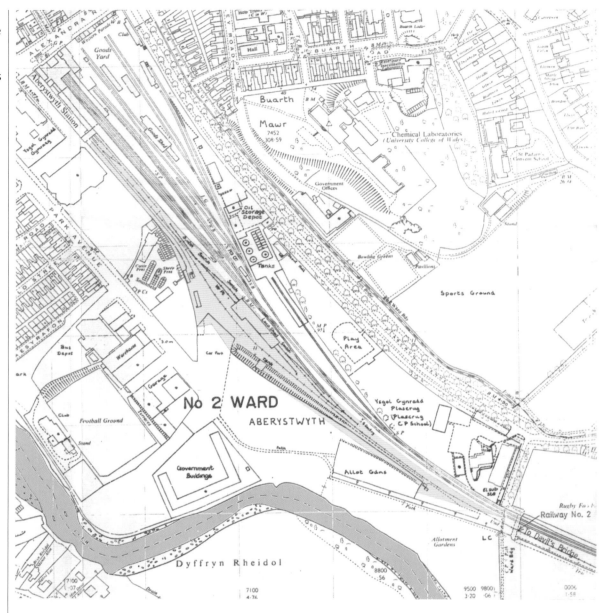

The deposited plan that accompanied the light railway order application covering the transfer of powers to a new owner and validating the 1968 realignment.

clauses dealing with axle loads and speeds contained in the 1898 light railway order were out of date and that the inspectorate required powers to amend them. The legal adviser also noted that the section on penalties for contraventions or failures to comply with provisions was also out of date.

The light railway order application was made, jointly by BR and the subsidiary company, on 22 August. A hiatus in its drafting had occurred in June, when BR's solicitor informed the Department of Transport that some 700 metres of the 1967/8 diversion was outside the limits of deviation and was a non-statutory railway. The proposed order, he wrote, implied that the entire line enjoyed statutory status and the eventual purchaser was entitled to expect that the railway had statutory authority and that defects should be remedied. He therefore proposed including provision to authorise that section to be worked as a light railway and subject to the 1897 Act and the 1902 Order. He could have commented that the old route had been abandoned without authority but did not.

Over 100 expressions of interest were received, identified by Lazards as potential purchasers. The author was one of them, and he certainly did not have any potential. Applicants who did included: Alton Towers Ltd, St Modwen Properties plc, Mostyn Estates, RFS Industries Ltd, RMC Group, Trafalgar House plc, Virgin Group (contact Richard Branson) and Venice-Simplon Orient Express Ltd.

Four bids were received:

and could provide the £400,000 working capital he said the railway would need.

The consortium said that it would operate the railway in accordance with the BR rule book, adopt BR engineering standards, keep the existing workforce and restore the railway to GWR condition as an independent minor railway.

The BMR was selected as the preferred bidder on 4 August 1988 and notified on 8 August.

Bidder	Bid	Net value of bid
Brecon Mountain Railway Limited	£306,500	£141,500
C.H. Eaves	£165,000	-
Oval (414) Limited (staff consortium)	£95,000 + £66,000	-£4,000
R.J. Harris	£10,500	-£154,500
The consortium had agreed to forego any redundancy benefits, valued by BR at £66,000. The net value of the bids was calculated by taking into account redundancy payments to the 18 persons likely to be affected by the sale, £150,000, £84,000 in the case of Oval (414) Limited, and site separation (fencing, gas and water supplies, re-siting a location cabinet) costs estimated at £15,000.		

The Brecon Mountain Railway (BMR) was then two miles long, established on a part of the Brecon & Merthyr Railway trackbed north of Merthyr Tydfil in 1980. In support of its application it explained that it had made a profit of £160,000, before taxes, on a turnover of £219,017 in 1987, and that it had received £548,500 in grants. Demonstrating the range of skills exploited in running the BMR, it said that it would improve the railway's shop and catering facilities and that it had further locomotives available to create further interest. Its bid related to the profitability it forecast would arise, it said, by its operations and added that substantial sums would have to be invested immediately to improve the railway.

A financier and stockbroker, Hugh Eaves was also the owner of Bury Football Club and a director of the Festiniog Railway Company; he said that he would run the railway with the support of volunteers and that investment of £500,000 would be required over the next five years.

Nothing is known about Harris; his bank reference said that he owned substantial assets

On hearing that it had not been successful, the staff consortium wrote to BR on 10 August, complaining that its bid had not been properly evaluated, that it had not been given an opportunity to improve its bid, and saying that it should have been given preference. On 23 August it also wrote to the local MP and to the town council, 'From our enquiries we know that our bid has not been read or fully understood by the BRB…' and appealed for help to achieve preferred bidder status.

At a meeting with BR on 5 September, the consortium restated its case for preference, following it up with a letter summarising its position the next day. It still wanted to acquire the railway, it was saddened that BR's decision was highly detrimental to its [BR's] public image, and it said that irrespective of the bid value the consortium's bid had many unique advantages – it did not identify them. If it had been allowed to meet the officer handling the disposal it could have established a rapport with him and the consortium would have saved money on professional advice. If BMR personnel visited the railway before the sale was complete, they should be escorted by a senior BR manager 'to avoid embarrassment'.

Another letter on 9 September 1988 alleged that the BMR had taken advantage of prior information about its bid. Around July 1987, the consortium had consulted the Great Little Trains of Wales Joint Marketing Panel (GLTW) and had been put in touch with the panel's treasurer, A.J. (Tony) Hills, the BMR's manager. Claiming that it had obtained assurances that the BMR was not interested in the railway, the consortium had given details of its proposals to Hills and now claimed that he had used the information to make BMR's bid.

When Lazard Brothers interviewed Hills and his business partner, Peter Rampton, about the allegations on 19 September a different picture emerged. On being told of the approach to the GLTW, Hills had suggested that it should issue a general statement to the effect that the railway should be kept open and jobs preserved. After GLTW had sent him, unsolicited, several pages of figures produced by the consortium, his response was that the organisation was not in a position to act as professional advisers and did not know much about the railway. Looking at the figures however, he saw errors, including a fundamental mistake regarding VAT. He told GLTW that he did not think much of the proposals and that it should adopt his proposal about a statement. When a consortium member telephoned him to complain about the lack of support he recommended that professional advice be obtained.

Hills and Rampton had first become interested in the railway in September 1987, when it appeared that scrap merchants were interested in it and that it might be broken up. They were interested in the locomotives and other items – Rampton had a large collection of narrow-gauge locomotives. They walked along part of the line and found it in better condition than expected.

Lazard Brothers and BR accepted that there had been no impropriety during the bidding process and that there was no agreement over the part the GLTW involvement might have played in the BMR formulating its bid. Both agreed that the BMR should continue as the preferred bidders. In letters to BR and in statements to the press the consortium continued making disparaging remarks about the BMR. *Private Eye*, published on 14 October 1988, had been told that if a train was derailed passengers faced a 400ft drop to their deaths and the only persons with sufficient skills to operate the line was the consortium or employees of the Ffestiniog or Snowdon Mountain railways. The consortium had valued the redundancy payments of its members at £205,000, somewhat more than BR's own calculation.

Notices of BR's intention to withdraw the train service had been published in the *Times* and *Daily Telegraph* on 22 June. They said that it was BRB's intention to seek a purchaser for the railway and that it would not implement the closure until a contract that provided for the continuance of services had become unconditional. The Transport Users Consultative Committee held an inquiry to hear objections in Aberystwyth on 13 December. It lasted 170 minutes.

Objections had been received from Dafydd Wigley MP, the NUR, two political parties, the Aberystwyth & District Trades Council and 13 individuals, including the actor Julie Christie. Ten of them attended or were represented at the inquiry. Two members of the consortium spoke on behalf of absent objectors, only one of them declaring his interest when he claimed that BRB had acted illegally because it had not offered the railway to the National Railway Museum as a historic relic under the terms of the Transport Act 1968, Section 144(7).

Only one objector complained of the hardship she would endure if the railway was closed, saying that she had to rely on friends when there were no trains during the winter. The BMR's Hills responded to complaints concerning loss of employment by saying that it was not intended to use volunteers.

The Committee submitted its report on 10 February 1989. It concluded that only a small number of people would experience hardship if the railway was closed, that it was essential that the railway continue to operate and everything possible done to maximise its value to tourism. However, it had reservations about the ability to impose the conditions of sale if the purchasing company failed. It asked the secretary of state to satisfy himself that the sale provided the best opportunity for ensuring that the railway would continue to operate in the longer term.

A problem had arisen with the sale, BR's solicitor informed the bid team on 3 October 1988. The BMR was concerned about the condition of the piles of the Rheidol river bridge and a retaining wall uphill from Rhiwfron. Either the purchase price should be renegotiated, or BR should agree to carry out the works. The civil engineer had surveyed the bridge in 1987, when it required repairs estimated to cost £30,000, and the retaining wall would cost £5,000. The solicitor recommended asking BMR for a contribution towards the cost of the repairs if they were undertaken by BR.

The BMR refused to countenance the works being carried out by BR and when the purchase agreement was signed on 7 October, and the deposit of £30,650 paid, BR agreed to pay up to £30,000 towards the bridge repairs subject to them being carried out within five years. BR also undertook to carry out closed-season maintenance as if it were not selling the railway while the BMR undertook to run a minimum service of two trains a day, six days a week on five consecutive months for at least five years. Reciprocal travel facilities for employees were to be provided for five years and the shares could not be sold within five years without approval being obtained from BR.

Solicitors acting for the consortium had tried to delay proceedings with a fax to Lazard Brothers on 6 October, saying that they had been appointed and that the exchange should be deferred until they had had time to be fully briefed about their clients' claims the following week. No comment on the request has been found; it appears to have been ignored. The consortium then tried to get BR to meet its expenses, treating an offer that BR would 'consider' contributing to them as a firm commitment. Peat Marwick McLintock, its accountants, claimed £10,000 on 28 November 1988 and its solicitors claimed £3,890 on 25 January 1989. On 16 March 1989 BR offered to make an ex gratia payment of £10,000 towards the expenses. Cheques for £3,000 and £7,000 were sent to the solicitors and Peat Marwick McLintock respectively on 25 April.

On 16 March the railway inspectorate's Major P.M. Olver had informed the Department of Transport that he was satisfied that the BMR was qualified to operate the railway in a safe and professional manner, that the terms of the amendment order were adequate to ensure that, and that he had always found the BMR to be in good condition and professionally operated when he had inspected it.

The sale was completed with a flurry of legal activity in March. The British Railways Llanbadarn (Vale of Rheidol) Level Crossing Order 1989 was made on 7 March and effective from 16 March. Made at the railway inspectorate's request and timed to ensure that the obligation to maintain and operate the crossing in accordance with its preferences was transferred to the new owner, the order details the protective equipment to be used and the conditions and requirements to be observed by the railway. An order for the parallel standard gauge crossing was made at the same time.

The ministerial decision on the application to close the railway prior

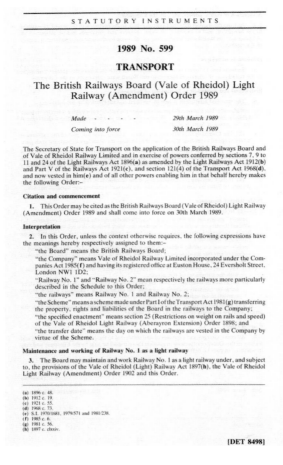

The 1989 amendment order.

The staff consortium's enamel pin badge, issued to mark its failed bid to buy the railway.

to its sale was published on 28 March, when consent was given to the closure. The scheme to transfer the assets to the company was made on 28 March with the vesting date set as 29 March. £98 of the company's share capital was issued to BRB on 29 March, when the minister gave his approval to the sale. The nominal cost of the transfer was £35,000, £100 share capital and £34,900 of non-interest-bearing unsecured loan stock. The latter was issued to BRB on 30 March.

Despite the objections made to the closure and sale, no objections were made to the light railway order so the British Railways Board (Vale of Rheidol) Light Railway (Amendment) Order 1989 was made on 29 March and put into effect on 30 March. The crucial point of the order was that it defined Railway No 1, the 1968 diversion and its associated land, as a light railway.

Finally, A.J. Hills and P.J. Rampton were appointed directors of Vale of Rheidol Railway Limited on 31 March. The BMR elected to pay 45% of the sale price immediately, deferring the remainder, and paying interest on it, until 31 July.

In just over 40 years of state ownership, the Vale of Rheidol Railway had survived, it seemed at times, against the odds. BR had tried its best, within the constraints placed upon it as the national railway operator, to develop the railway as a late 20th Century tourist railway. But the condition of the line in 1989 showed that it had been unable to devote sufficient resources to it. While that might appear to be failure it had run the railway longer than any previous owner and until an owner with the resources and focus that it deserved could be found to take it on. Events have shown that that its buyer could be trusted to care for the railway and to take it forward.

In a final gesture of defiance the staff consortium commissioned the manufacture of an enamel pin badge illustrated with a train and inscribed 'Sold down the Rheidol.'

CHAPTER 5

PRIVATISATION – RETURN TO INDEPENDENCE

The end of the BR era had been marked on 5 November 1988 with a bonfire night special that was met by fireworks at the stations and a Santa special on 18 December. The 31st of March 1989 being a Friday, the Brecon Mountain Railway took over the railway from 3 April; Aberystwyth booking office staff handed over the keys in silence.

BR had not done too well out of the sale. Information prepared for a response to a Parliamentary question released on 12 June 1989 states that the direct costs had been £314,000, resulting in a cash loss of £7,500, although the costs of any redundancies were then unknown. It was pointed out that BR would also make savings in future years. The note did not comment on the commitment to pay the BMR £53,000 for the outstanding work (Appendix 20).

Later, one of the invoices was refused by BR's accounts department, so on 29 August 1989 A.J. Hills informed BR that the final sale payment due on 31 July had been deposited with the BMR's solicitors pending settlement of the outstanding invoices. The impasse was soon resolved.

The sale agreement clause covering the sale of the company's shares was put into effect in 1990, when the BMR sought and obtained approval to sell them to the Phyllis Rampton Narrow Gauge Railway Trust, a charity founded by Peter Rampton in 1985. The transfer was completed on 11 December 1990 and the commercial relationship with the BMR was ended in November 1996. On 10 April 1995 the Charity Commissioners had advised the trust that its arrangements with the railway were not acceptable within the objectives and regulations governing its conduct, the outcome

being that the railway company was registered as a charity on 16 June 1999.

The trust's role is to fund the restoration of heritage assets, but it loans the company match-funding for grant-aided projects as well. Otherwise the company is expected to fund its development from profits.

In one sense, the new owners continued to operate the railway in the same way that BR had attempted, as a commercial line without volunteer input. In another it was very different, in that initially their priority was to concentrate on the line's infrastructure, rather than marketing. Terry Turner, former operating manager of the Ffestiniog Railway, was appointed to manage the railway and train services started on 21 May 1989. Turner was replaced by Neil Thompson in 1992. Members of the supporters' association transferred their allegiance, and their assets, to the Welshpool & Llanfair Light Railway.

For passengers, perhaps the most noticeable difference in the change in ownership came when they bought tickets at Aberystwyth. Instead of using the standard gauge booking hall, they used one of the brake vans stabled in the headshunt and then a wooden building located on the Manchester & Milford Railway platform. Later a sales counter was located there too. At Devil's Bridge loco crews were instructed to leave their steeds in the headshunt while they took their breaks, so passengers could take photographs, instead of running round straight away and hiding the loco out of sight by the water tank.

On the track, the first priority was to eliminate the use of rail spikes, a target that was achieved by 1995. Since then most of the track has been replaced with

A train high above the Rheidol valley during 1989, the first season of privatisation. No 7 retains its BR smokebox numberplate brackets.

Seen on 20 August 1992 No 7 is equipped with air brakes and lays over in the headshunt at Devil's Bridge for passengers to take photographs.

second-hand 75lb or new 60lb rail. The loops at Aberffrwd and Capel Bangor were reinstated in 1990, using turnouts from the east end of the loco shed, and 2001 respectively. Renewal of the Rheidol river bridge was carried out over the winter of 1991/2 at a cost of £105,077, the cheque for £30,000 due to the BMR being issued by BR on 7 April 1992. Storage sheds were erected at Capel Bangor in 2004 and 2018.

No 9 was sent to the BMR's workshop at Pant, Merthyr Tydfil, to be overhauled on 19 May 1989, returning to service in maroon livery and equipped with air brakes in July 1991. The change in braking system was adopted because the vacuum brake equipment inherited from BR was worn out and expensive to replace. Air braking systems have the advantage of using standard components used in road vehicles that are cheap and easy to obtain. Using less steam to operate, they reduce operating costs too. It does have to be said, however, that the Polish air pump attached to the left-hand water tank was not universally welcomed by enthusiasts.

The loco was returned to the BMR in November and used on that railway's Santa trains during December.

No 7 was equipped with air-brake equipment at Aberystwyth in 1992 and No 8 was despatched to be overhauled at Pant in May 1993 and returned to Aberystwyth on 6 July 1996, painted in GWR livery.

Six carriages were equipped with air brakes in 1991, and six more in 1992, when the 12 vehicles ran in GWR chocolate and cream with the addition of original-style crests.

A setback occurred in April 1996, with the discovery of another landslip at the Alltddu site, where there had been a slip in 1978. This time a more substantial repair was carried out, concrete plug with 30-40 cubic metres of concrete, a task hampered by the site's remoteness and being on land designated a Site of Special Scientific Interest. A tunnelling car was hired to ferry ready-mixed concrete from Nantyronen, and five skips hired from the Ffestiniog Railway carried 400 tons of spoil from the site up to Devil's Bridge. While the work was in progress passenger trains were run

By 1 June 1997 No 7's appearance has been enhanced by a modicum of lining and the addition of an original company transfer on its cabsides. With a contribution from BR, the bridge had been renewed in 1991/2. The area is a popular spot with locals for dog walking, sunbathing or fooling about in the river. The author has no evidence to support a story that students enjoyed 'smoking' under the bridge.

Nos 8 and 9 passing at the reinstated Aberffrwd loop in 1991. No 8 and its train retain their vacuum brakes. No 9 had only been returned from being overhauled at the Brecon Mountain Railway a few weeks before. The cut-outs in its buffer plank were to act as jacking points in the event of derailment. The feature was applied to all three locos but has now been concealed to restore the original appearance.

No 9 during its brief sojourn on the Brecon Mountain Railway, leaving Pant with the first Santa train of the day on 20 December 1992. Another feature of the BMR rebuild, applied to both Nos 8 and 9, was positioning the cab handrails outside.

Taking water at Devil's Bridge on 4 August 1996. No 8 had been returned from its overhaul at the Brecon Mountain Railway on 6 July. The GWR installed the water tank in 1924.

A mixed train run for photographers with newly-overhauled No 8 on 4 August 1996.

Work in progress to stabilise the ground at the Alltddu mine site, seen on 9 June 1996.

as far as Aberffrwd, but half the traffic was lost, and all of that originating at Devil's Bridge. The line reopened on 18 June.

Another setback, two level crossing accidents in 1997, arose from an unkept promise and brought a change to the railway's infrastructure at Glanyrafon. When Dyfed County Council had started to develop the area as an industrial estate in 1980 it built an access road across the railway from the A44, promising BR that it would pay for the crossing to be automated if the traffic required it. A review in 1995 had recommended that the work be done, but the scheme was overlooked during a period of local authority reorganisation limbo.

The incidents, which occurred on 26 April, when three people were injured, and on 9 December, when a works train was derailed, brought matters to a head and the railway inspectorate insisted that the work be carried out. The Vale of Rheidol Railway Glanyrafon level crossing order 2000 was made on 5 September 2000, effective from 17 September, giving authority to the £130,000 scheme completed

at council expense. The railway received £27,500 in respect of future maintenance. No action was taken to implement the inspectorate's requirement to fit the locomotives with flashing amber beacons.

Restoration of a loco from the railway's museum collection was completed in 2002. Kerr, Stuart 'Wren' 0-4-0ST No 3114 had been acquired in 1998 and was restored by trustee Allen Civil at his Staffordshire home. It was hired to the Devon Railway Centre for 18 months from 2010.

Despite the limited resources available at Aberystwyth the railway was capable of producing some solidly engineered equipment to support its track maintenance programme. A ballast plough completed in 2003 was followed by the adaptation of a diesel locomotive to create a self-propelled hedge-trimmer/mowing machine in 2007. Seven restored four-wheeled wagons, two South African bogie ballast hopper wagons and a self-propelled tamping machine were also in service by 2003.

The idea of developing a museum to house Rampton's collection at Aberystwyth was floated quite soon after the purchase

No 7 crossing the Glanyrafon industrial estate road on 20 August 1992. The location was originally known as Glanrafon.

A contrasting view of the same loco at the same site on 14 September 2019.

The museum collection's Kerr, Stuart 'Wren' 0-4-0ST No 3114 made its first public appearance after restoration at Staffordshire's Amerton Railway on 28 April 2002. On the footplate are Allan Civil, who restored it in his garage, and Neil Thompson, then the railway's general manager.

To aid track renewals and maintenance this 1985-built Plasser tamper was bought from its South African maker in 1991. It was seen returning to Aberystwyth after working up the line on 29 May 1999.

and additions since 1998 were sent to Capel Bangor for storage. Ownership of the remainder of the collection was transferred to the company in 2003. In 2004 the Heritage Lottery Fund rejected the first of several applications for financial support but in June 2010 the Welsh Assembly Government announced that it would make a £300,000 contribution towards a £1.1 million project to develop a restoration/ training workshop at Aberystwyth. Construction was started in 2011.

The 180ft x 60ft building is located on the site of the standard gauge water tower/coaling stage demolished in 1996. It contains a fully equipped machine shop, a carriage restoration bay, staff facilities and an overhead gantry crane. A locomotive running shed is provided at the west end of the building. Although some aspects of the building were incomplete, the workshop was used from January 2015, and the locos were moved into the running shed in 2018.

From 2012, passenger facilities were improved by moving the shop and booking office to a position close to the car park. The Manchester & Milford Railway platform was also demolished and replaced by a platform that was suitable for use with narrow-gauge trains; it was used for the first time on 3 April. In 2013 a canopy was erected to provide an undercover passenger waiting area.

In 2012 the railway had secured a Ceredigion County Council-administered European Regional Development Fund grant to reinstate the buildings at the intermediate stations, except Llanbadarn, the railway hoping that passengers could be encouraged to leave the train and explore the Rheidol valley. The original buildings had fallen into disrepair and had been demolished by British Railways.

Another development in 2012 arose from rising oil prices, leading to the conversion of No 8 back to coal firing. No 9 was converted in 2013, re-entering

This self-propelled flail is based on an-ex Ministry of Defence Hunslet 2ft 6in gauge diesel locomotive, built in 1977. Acquired in 1999, it was converted at Aberystwyth and is seen in action at Llanbadarn in June 2018.

In 1998-2000 several additions to the museum collection were displayed at Aberystwyth before under-cover storage could be provided for them. (Peter Heath)

The loco shed looking east on 20 August 1992, a view that has changed considerably. After the coaling stage, with its roof top water tank, was demolished, the water column by the shed door was replaced by a tank mounted on a plinth. The wagons coupled to the diesel locomotive originated from the Plynlimon & Hafan Railway and have been extensively rebuilt over the years. The other wagon is one of those acquired from the Midland Railway Carriage & Wagon Company.

No 1213 passes the new running shed and workshop building as it returns to Aberystwyth on 10 June 2018. Land to the right of the workshop is earmarked for a museum that will incorporate beams from the roof of London Bridge station.

The Rheidol Falls platform under construction as seen from the train on 16 February 2013. This was the first year that trains were run during the February half-term.

Before it was returned to its original appearance, with concealed air pump and GWR livery, No 9 ran for a few months in a variant of the GWR livery that it carried before Nationalisation. It is seen at Capel Bangor on 26 September 2015, after the station building had been reinstated and the platforms constructed.

service on 26 April. The sale of the oil storage tank covered the cost of converting the locos.

Operations in 2012 were affected by heavy rain flooding the line between Llanbadarn and Glanrafon and overtopping the river bridge on 9 June, leading to services being suspended. The next day an embankment was found to

have been washed away at Glanrafon, leaving 15ft of track suspended up to 2ft in the air. Services were restored on 15 June.

The operation of Santa trains to Capel Bangor in December 2012, the first operated since privatisation, proved to be a great success, with extra trains run to meet demand and extra capacity required each year since. Electric heating and lighting were installed in the train, powered by a generator located in the brake van. Another first was the operation of trains during the February half-term holiday in 2013.

Neil Thompson, the railway's general manager since 1992, left in December 2012 and was replaced by Llyr Ap Iolo, an engineer with 25 years footplate experience on the Ffestiniog and Welsh Highland Railways.

An indication of the scale of the railway's ambition for its museum came in May 2013, with the announcement that it had secured components from the barrel arch roof of London Bridge station, a listed structure dating from 1866, to be incorporated into it.

Another view that has changed at Aberystwyth, seen on 4 August 1996. The back of the train is passing the site of the new workshop building while No 8 is passing the site of the new passenger platform. Bunded with Braithwaite panels, the tank wagon was sold for a good price when the railway's use of oil as a locomotive fuel came to an end.

Burning coal again, No 8 pulls into Aberffrwd, 16 February 2013.

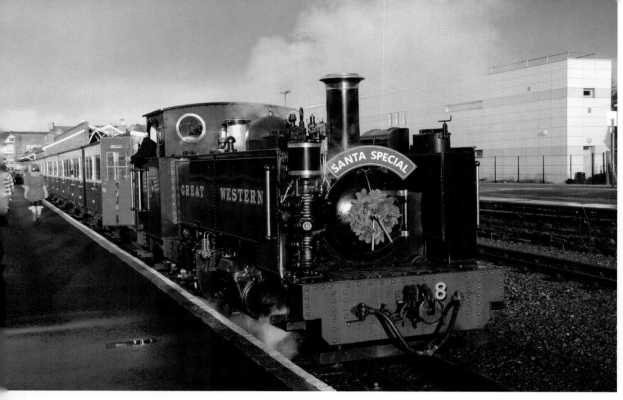

On 15 December 2012 the railway returned to the Santa train market for the first time since BR had run its last trains in 1988. In this incarnation they ran as far as Capel Bangor, proving extremely popular and calling for increased capacity each year since. Here the train is seen at the lowered platform that avoided passengers having to board from the ground.

Devil's Bridge in 2014, with its new platform and 'driver for a fiver' track, complete with loco shed. Installation of the platform gas lights has since been completed, restoring a feature of the station as it once was. The railway built a car park in the field on the right in 2019.

Phyllis Rampton
Narrow Gauge
Railway Trust founder
Peter Rampton
addresses the guests
attending the event
that marked the
completion of the
stations project at
Aberffrwd on 19 June
2014.

They have been placed in store until the time comes to proceed with the building.

In August 2013, passengers found a new attraction at Devil's Bridge, in the form of the railway's Kerr, Stuart 'Wren' 0-4-0ST No 3114 running on an isolated siding and offering 'driver for a fiver' sessions, the revenue contributing to the loco's maintenance.

In 2014 the station's gas lighting was restored, using authentic cast iron standards and a bottled gas supply.

Passengers' views from the trains were improved following the creation of eleven 50-100m 'viewing windows' on a two-mile stretch of the line between Rheidol Falls Halt and Devil's Bridge in 2014. Carried out in partnership with Natural Resources Wales, the work required around 250 trees to be felled, enabling new, natural growth, including flowers and native ash trees, to develop.

Running in maroon since it was overhauled at the Brecon Mountain Railway in 1991, No 9 was repainted in Cambrian Railways livery in 2014, celebrating that railway's 150th anniversary. The livery change was short-lived, GWR livery being applied and

its original number, 1213, reinstated, in 2015. This was the first showing for the railway's strategy of running all its stock in original livery, a development that required removal of the names applied to the locomotives by British Railways in 1956. The carriages had been restored or repainted in full GWR livery, with GWR fleet numbers reinstated, since 2013.

Completion of the grant-aided stations project was marked by the operation of a special double-headed train on 19 June 2014. At Aberffrwd, chief guest Edwina Hart AM, Welsh government minister for economy, science and transport, was introduced to guests by Peter Rampton, founder of the trust that has owned the railway since 1990. Alongside the stations project, a station support volunteer group was founded, which looks after their gardens and other lineside features.

The railway's first enthusiast event since BR days took place over two weekends in September 2014, with operation of the Ffestiniog Railway's England 0-4-0ST *Palmerston*, which had been hired to the railway 100 years before, proving a major attraction.

Commissioning of the new workshop in January 2015 was marked by the announcement of a £288,000 Coastal Communities Fund award. Under the heading 'our past is their future' the award funded additional machinery and specialist tools, developing a training school and engineering business, employing two engineers and four additional apprentices, and starting the restoration of 2-6-2T No 7 which had been out of service since 1998. The fund receives income from the Crown Estate's marine assets and is administered by the Big Lottery Fund. Before work started on No 7, No 8 received a mechanical overhaul.

After the railway made it known that workshop capacity would be made available to other railways or locomotive owners it was rewarded with orders. In 2015 it completed the restoration of Kerr, Stuart 0-4-0T *Diana* for a private owner alongside the completion of the restoration of the museum collection's Hunslet 0-4-0ST *Margaret*. In 2017/8 it overhauled the Talyllyn Railway's ex-Corris Railway Hughes 0-4-2ST No 3 *Sir Haydn*. Later in 2018 work was started on the restoration of a Baldwin 2-6-2T for Welsh Highland Railway Ltd. In 2016 *Margaret* moved on to 'driver for a fiver' duty at Devil's Bridge, allowing Kerr, Stuart 0-4-0ST No 3114 to be hired to the London Museum of Water & Steam at Kew Bridge.

When No 7's overhaul was completed in October 2018, the three 2-6-2Ts had the same livery for the first time since 1982 and were available for use for the first time in 20 years. Following a trial with No 8 in 2017, No 7's air pump was concealed in a compartment built into the left-hand water tank, restoring their original outline. The same modification will be applied to No 1213 when its tanks are renewed. No 7 was run in on the Santa trains in December 2018, and formally entered service on 16 February 2019. Modifications to the

Palmerston, visiting from the Ffestiniog Railway, and No 9 in its short-lived Cambrian livery crossing at Aberffrwd on 21 September 2014.

A view of the machine shop in the new workshop building.

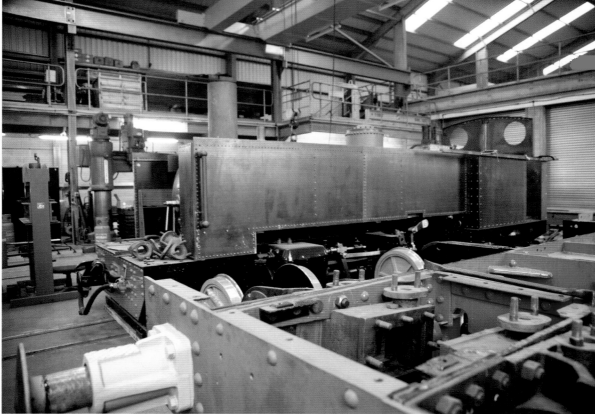

The restoration of No 7 was at an advanced stage when photographed on 19 December 2017. In the foreground are the frames of the Talyllyn Railway's Hughes 0-4-2ST No 3, whose overhaul was a contract job by the railway.

buffer beams, cab handrails, chimney caps and roof rain strips made in the interest of reinstating original features had also been trialled on No 8. One altered feature that remained was the increased cab height, retained in the interest of crew comfort.

Two summer cars were returned to service, modified to improve access for disabled travellers, in 2018. The first of them was No 4999, which had been BR's 'vista car' in 1983. Due to its weight and lack of ventilation it had not been a success in this form and had been out of service since 1989. Its entry into service was marked by an event on 11 June. The Coastal Communities Fund had made a £250,000 grant that funded the supervision of two apprentices to carry out the work, and to install accessible 1st class accommodation to two other vehicles. A £5,000 award from the Big Lottery Fund contributed to the cost of restoring a GWR cattle van that had been obtained from the Ffestiniog Railway.

On the railway, in June and July 2018, services were suspended for two weeks when lineside fires during a period of hot weather forced it to close. Fencing and sleepers needed replacing before services could be resumed. The railway was not implicated in the fires, the cause remaining unknown.

After many years of planning, the railway ended 2018 by announcing that it had obtained funding for the development of Aberystwyth station and was about to start work. £1.6 million of the £2.4 million project cost was a grant from a European Union fund managed by the Welsh Government's Tourism Attractor Destination programme. The same programme made a substantial contribution to the Welsh Highland Railway's Caernarfon station.

To be phased over three years, the first stage was completed in February 2019, with a coal store, ashing-out pit and water tank improving loco operating facilities, and, for passengers, a new platform and

Kerr, Stuart 0-4-0T *Diana* and Hunslet 0-4-0ST *Margaret* passing Llanbadarn on 26 September 2015. The completion of *Diana*'s restoration was the first contract job carried out in the new workshop. *Margaret* was acquired for the museum collection in a partially restored condition in 1999 and was completed alongside *Diana*. Neither had been steamed for more than 40 years.

The completion of No 7's overhaul in October 2018, 20 years since it had been withdrawn, provided an opportunity to display the three locomotives together, in the same livery, for the first time since 1956.

The former vista car, No 4999, restored to original condition with modification to improve access, at Devil's Bridge on 11 June 2018.

On 16 February 2019 No 7 leaves Aberystwyth with its first train to Devil's Bridge since the completion of its overhaul. It was also the first departure from the new Aberystwyth platform, the railway's fourth station in the town. The building on the left was a temporary booking office and shop. The building with a pagoda roof is a toilet block, the first permanent facilities the railway has ever provided for its passengers at Aberystwyth.

toilets alongside the car park. Future stages will see the erection of a shop and booking office, a three-road carriage storage and maintenance shed on the site of the 1968 station, construction of a café and the conversion of the GWR loco shed into a 5,000sq ft multi-function display area and event space. The station's ambiance will be that of a 1930s GWR development, with corrugated iron cladding and pagoda-style roofs, but built to twenty-first century standards.

The world today is very different to the one known by the Vale of Rheidol Railway's promoters, who could not have imagined that the fruits of their labours would still be in existence over 100 years later. Not only that, but capable of attracting financial support from public authorities, and in better condition, and better equipped, than they ever knew. With the support of the trust and the railway's vibrant and dedicated management and staff, it is clear that the Vale

of Rheidol Railway is in a sound position and there is every reason to expect that to endure.

Peter Rampton, who funded the railway's purchase from British Rail in 1989, died on 22 July 2019, aged 85. A man who ploughed his own furrow, he was determined that everything the railway did should be to the highest possible standards. He will inspire the railway's direction for many years to come.

LOCOMOTIVES

No 1 2-6-2T *Edward VII* Davies & Metcalf 1902, name removed 1912, No 1212 from 1922, scrapped 1935

No 2 2-6-2T *Prince of Wales* Davies & Metcalf 1902, name removed 1912, scrapped c1924

No 3 2-4-0T *Rheidol* Bagnall 1497/1897, name removed 1912, scrapped 1924

No 7 2-6-2T Swindon 1923, named *Owain Glyndwr* 1956, name removed 2018

No 8 2-6-2T Swindon 1923, named *Llewelyn* 1956, name removed 2014

No 1213 2-6-2T Swindon 1924, nominally, but not actually, a rebuild of No 2, No 9 from 1948, named *Prince of Wales* 1956, No 1213 restored and name removed 2016

No 10 0-6-0DH Brecon Mountain Railway 1987, constructed using Baguley components

Museum Collection

Builder	Works Number	Name	Date	Wheel Arrangement	Gauge	Number	Notes
A Borsig	5913		1908	0-4-0WT	600mm		Sobemai N.V. Maldegem, Belgium
Franco-Belge	2668		1951	2-8-2	2ft	121	SAR NG15 Class, South Africa
De Winton	106	*Kathleen*	1877	0-4-0VBT	1ft 10¾in	1877	Penrhyn Quarry
Decauville	1027		1926	0-4-0T	597mm	7	Belgian Industries, Pas-De-Calais, France.
Falcon	265		1897	4-4-0	2ft	27	Beira Railway 'Lawley' via Buzi Sugar Refinery, Mozambique
Falcon	266	*Lisboa*	1897	4-4-0	2ft	28	Beira Railway 'Lawley' via Buzi Sugar Refinery, Mozambique
Fowler	10249		1905	0-6-0	1ft 11¾in	6	Central Sugar, Lautoka, Fiji
Fowler	11938		1909	0-4-2T	1ft 11⅝in	S.S.E 21	Sena Sugar, Mozambique
Fowler	15515		1920	0-6-2T	1ft 11⅝in	S.S.E 23	Sena Sugar, Mozambique
Henschel	11854		1925		597mm	1917	Bogie tender for Feldbahn locomotives.
Hudswell, Clarke	D564		1930	4wDM	2ft		Hindlow quarries.
Hunslet	605	*Margaret*	1894	0-4-0T	1ft 11¾in		Penrhyn Quarry
Kerr, Stuart	3114		1918	0-4-0T	1ft 11⅝in		Wren Class
Kerr, Stuart	4408		1928	0-6-4T	2ft 6in	695	Parlakimidi Light Railway, India
Maffei	4766		1916	0-8-0	597mm	DFB 968/31	Deutscher Feldbahn
North British	17111		1906	4-6-0T	2ft 6in	666	Parlakimidi Light Railway, India
Ruston, Proctor	50823 or 51168		1915 or 1916	4wPM	1,000mm		Oldest narrow gauge internal combustion loco in British Isles. Cotton Powder Company
Sabero	6	*La Herrera*	1937	0-6-0T	600mm	6	Hulleras de sabero y Anexas S.A., Spain
Bagnall	2228		1924	0-4-4T	2ft	18BG	Sha Tau Kok Railway, Hong Kong via Victorias Milling Co., Philippines
Bagnall	2192	*Conqueror*	1922	0-6-2T	2ft 6in	3	Bowater's Railway, Kent
Bagnall	2029		1916	2-6-2T	2ft 6in	AK16	Kalighat Falta Railway, Calcutta, India
Bagnall	2457		1932	4-6-2	2ft	38	Gwalior Railway, India.
Bagnall	2460		1932	4-6-2	2ft	41	Gwalior Railway, India

VALE OF RHEIDOL LIGHT RAILWAY SHARE CAPITAL

	Date	Amount created	Amount received	Calls in arrears	Uncalled
Ordinary £10 shares	December 1901	£51,000	£26,890	£13,910	£9,250
Ordinary £10 shares	June 1902	£51,000	£44,140	£6,860	
Ordinary £10 shares	December 1902	£51,000	£51,000		
4% debentures	December 1902	£16,900	£16,900		

The untidy state of the ground is indicative of this photograph *Edward VII* and train at Aberystwyth being taken before the railway was opened. Manager James Rees's office building is seen in its original position at the end of the line. (Michael Bishop collection)

CAPITAL EXPENDITURE 1901/2

	June 1901	December 1901	June 1902	December 1902
Construction contract, on account	£9,363 2s 4d	£16,540 0s 0d	£16,016 10s 0d	£12,288 11s 3d
Locomotive account			£1,000 0s 0d	£1,755 0s 0d
Land purchase		£375 16s 1d	£76 14s 2d	
Rent of office, expenses		£263 18s 7d	£279 14s 2d	
Engineering fees		£763 0s 0d	£300 0s 0d	£787 0s 0d
Rolling stock – trucks		£137 0s 0d	£137 10s 0d	
Signalling & telegraphs			£450 0s 0d	
Travelling expenses		£13 14s 0d	£26 16s 10d	
Printing, stationery and stamps		£5 8s 6d	£8 5s 5d	
Law charges		12s 6d		
Auditors		£5 5s 0d	£5 5s 0d	£5 5s 0d
General charges, including expenses to date of opening				£358 3s 0d
Interest on paid-up capital		£76 18s 1d	£87 8s 6d	£60 3s 3d
Legal expenses, stamps and brokerages				£1,721 4s 3d
Traffic superintendent's department expenses			£45 8s 10d	
	£9,363 2s 4d	£18,182 2s 9d	£18,433 11s 11d	£16,975 6s 9d
Less interest received		£4 19s 9d		
		£18,177 3s 0d		

CONSTRUCTION EXPENDITURE

	31 December 1901	30 June 1902	31 December 1902
Contract – payment on account	£16,540	£16,016 10s	£12,288 11s 3d
Works			
Locomotive account		£1,000	£1,755
Land purchase	£375 16s 1d	£76 14s 2d	
Rent of offices	£263 18s 7d	£279 14s 2d	
Engineering fees	£763	£300	£787
Rolling stock – trucks	£137 10s	£137 10s	
Signalling and telegraph		£450	
Travelling expenses	£13 14s	£26 15s 10d	
Printing, stationery and stamps	£5 8s 6d	£8 5s 5d	
Law charges	£0 12s 6d		£1,721 4s 3d
Auditors	£5 5s	£5 5s	£5 5s
Interest on capital	£76 18s 1d	£87 8s 6d	£60 3s 3d
Traffic superintendent's department expenses		£45 8s 10d	
General charges, including expenses to date of opening			£358 3s
Land and compensation			
	£18,182 2s 9d		
Less interest received	£4 19s 9d		
	£18,177 3s	£18,433 11s 11d	£16,975 6s 9d

CAPITAL EXPENDITURE 1903-10

	1903	1904	1905	1906	1907	1908	1910
Works	£277 3s 5d						
Law charges	£250						
General charges, including expenses to date of opening	£1,055 5s						
Land and compensation	£34	£127 3s	£19 17s		£94 15s 3d	£88 10s 2d	£76 17s 8d
Working stock	£3,845 11s 9d						
Devil's Bridge – erecting girder bridge	£16 16s 7d	£2 3s 4d					
Nantyronen – water tank	£8 15s 6d	£14 13s 3d					
Plascrug – Cambrian siding, contribution to cost	£26						
Rhiwfron – points and levers fixed at siding	£8 7s 6d						
Aberystwyth – telephone equipment and works	£38 3s 11d						
Purchase of locomotive *Rheidol*	£591						
Retentions, locomotives and carriages	£271 11s 8d						
Additions to carriages	£1 3s 1d	£8 3s 2d					
Engineering settlement		£40					
Aberffrwd – passing place and station		£255 7s 10d					
Glanrafon – stopping place		£2 11s 2d					
Sundry equipment		£35 8s 6d					
Seats for station platforms		£9					
Lamps for Aberffrwd		£1 11s 6d					
Weighbridge at Devil's Bridge			£54 5s				
Foundations for weighbridge at Devil's Bridge			£15 15s 7d				
First class seating for carriages			£45 11s 8d				
Six box wagons			£252				
One ton derrick crane for Devil's Bridge				£20			
Further first class seating for carriages				£22 15s 10d			
	£6,423 18s 5d	£496 1s 10d	£387 9s 3d	£42 15s 10d	£94 15s 3d	£88 10s 2d	£76 17s 8d

BOARD OF TRADE RETURNS

	1903	1904	1905	1906	1907	1908	1909	1910	1911	1912	1913
Authorised capital											
Shares/stock	£51,000	£51,000	£51,000	£51,000	£51,000	£51,000	£51,000	£51,000	£51,000	£51,000	£51,000
Loans/debentures	£17,000	£17,000	£17,000	£17,000	£17,000	£17,000	£17,000	£17,000	£17,000	£17,000	£17,000
Aberayron extension											
Shares/stock	£63,000	£63,000	£63,000	£63,000	£63,000	£63,000	£63,000	£63,000	£63,000	£63,000	£63,000
Loans/debentures	£21,000	£21,000	£21,000	£21,000	£21,000	£21,000	£21,000	£21,000	£21,000	£21,000	£21,000
Issued											
Shares/stock	£51,000	£51,000	£51,000	£51,000	£51,000	£51,000	£51,000	£51,000	£51,000	£51,000	£51,000
Debentures 4%	£16,900	£16,900	£16,900	£16,900	£16,900	£16,900	£16,900	£16,900	£16,900	£16,900	£16,900
Capital expenditure	£6,083	£496	£387		£95	£88					
Dividend	1.50%	1.50%	1.50%	1.50%	1.25%		1.25%	0.75%	0.75%	0.75%	0.50%
Passengers carried											
First class			801	2,941	2,777	1,695	1,909	1,016	1,972	2,140	
Third class	103,072	101,674	104,967	97,809	107,257	101,370	105,429	125,342	116,396	117,438	
			105,768	100,750	110,034	103,065	107,338	126,358	118,368	119,578	31,215
Season tickets		2	1	1							
Goods, mineral and livestock traffic											
Merchandise (tons)	1,238	1,115	1,613	1,792	1,672	1,284	1,094	741	860	1,481	
Coal, coke and patent fuel (tons)											
Minerals (tons)	4,049	4,858	5,259	5,783	4,715	4,965	3,291	2,831	3,412	2,906	
Train miles											
Passenger	31,008	31,753	34,249	34,295	35,237	37,326	36,851	34,942	34,050	34,460	14,085
Goods	5,923	3,814	4,096	6,848	4,563	2,910	1,403	1,567	1,751	1,946	882
Ballast	3,448	1,816	958	1,629	1,832	852	129	69	420	180	155
Total	40,379	37,383	39,303	42,772	41,632	41,088	38,383	36,578	36,221	36,586	15,122
Revenue receipts											
Passengers											
First class			£108	£203	£190	£181	£123	£110	£122	£129	£33
Third class	£3,703	£3,886	£3,790	£3,620	£3,745	£3,572	£3,889	£4,075	£4,079	£4,078	£938
Season tickets		£17	£15	£15							£5
Total receipts from passengers	£3,703	£3,903	£3,913	£3,838	£3,935	£3,753	£4,012	£4,185	£4,201	£4,207	£976
Parcels under 2cwt and excess luggage	£82	£98	£31	£27	£30	£33	£37	£32	£63	£134	£30
Mails and parcel post				£15	£60	£60	£60	£60	£60	£60	£55
Total passenger train receipts	£3,785	£4,001	£3,944	£3,880	£4,025	£3,846	£4,109	£4,277	£4,324	£4,401	£1,061
Goods train traffic											
Merchandise	£143	£191	£371	£560	£465	£386	£346	£250	£330	£475	£150

	1903	1904	1905	1906	1907	1908	1909	1910	1911	1912	1913
Livestock				£9	£10						
Coal, coke, etc											£52
Minerals	£662	£745	£627	£662	£547	£613	£374	£316	£393	£308	£144
Total goods train receipts	£805	£936	£998	£1,231	£1,022	£999	£720	£566	£723	£783	£346
Miscellaneous	£113	£188	£211	£119	£99	£61	£67	£22	£21	£22	£1
Traffic revenue	£4,703	£5,125	£5,153	£5,230	£5,146	£4,906	£4,896	£5,431	£5,068	£5,206	£1,408
Revenue expenditure											
Maintenance of way and works	£219	£794	£911	£885	£901	£884	£893	£496	£1,085	£905	£371
Maintenance of rolling stock	£92	£151	£199	£196	£88	£189	£120	£139	£182	£105	£263
Loco running expenses	£1,057	£1,253	£1,368	£1,367	£1,672	£1,581	£1,483	£1,354	£1,361	£1,367	£651
Traffic expenses	£761	£759	£762	£776	£707	£727	£652	£716	£742	£787	£372
General charges	£598	£285	£268	£309	£297	£317	£303	£342	£254	£374	£14
Rents and rates	£78	£85	£78	£1	£91	£95	£94	£102	£113	£111	£75
Compensation – personal injury	£2	£64	£38	£46	£51	£51	£51	£4	£58	£6	£19
Damage and loss of goods, property, &c		£4	£32	£10							£17
Legal and Parliamentary				£56				£24		£375	
Miscellaneous		£3	£3		£19	£27	£21		£3	£8	£40
Total expenditure	£2,807	£3,398	£3,659	£3,646	£3,826	£3,871	£3,617	£3,177	£3,798	£4,038	£1,822
Total receipts	£4,703	£5,125	£5,153	£5,230	£1,546	£4,906	£4,896	£5,216	£5,068	£5,206	£1,412
Net receipts	£1,896	£1,727	£1,494	£1,584	£1,320	£1,035	£1,279	£2,039	£1,270	£1,168	-£410
Ratio expenditure/receipts	60%	66%	71%	70%	74%	79%	74%	61%	75%	78%	129%
Rolling stock											
Steam locomotives	3	3	3	3	3	3	3	3	3	3	3
Passenger carriages	12	12	12	12	12	12	12	12	12	12	12
Other coaching vehicles	3	3	3	3	3	3	3	3	3	3	3
Merchandise and mineral vehicles	18	18	23	23	23	23	23	23	23	23	23

EMPLOYEES 1910

Number of men	Trade	Rate per day	Per week (six days)
3	Gangers	1 @ 5s 5d; 1 @ 3s 6d; 1 @ 3s 4d	£3 13s 6d
8	Platelayers	All @ 2s 10d	£6 16s
1	Carpenter	4s 1d	£1 4s 6d
2	Drivers	1 @ 5s 4d; 1 @ 4s 2d	£2 17s
2	Firemen	1 @ 3s 4d; 1 @ 3s	£1 18s
1	Cleaner	3s	18s
1	Fitter	5s 8d	£1 14s
1	Painter	3s 9d	£1 2s 6d
3	Station masters	1 @ 4s 5d; 1 @ 3s 9d; 1 @ 2s 9d	£3 5s 6d
2	Clerks in charge	1s	12s
1	Porter	1s 8d	10s
3	Guards	1 @ 3s 6d; 1 @ 2s 11d; 1 @ 1s 8d	£2 8s 6d
1	Transhipper	3s 2d	19s
1	Clerk	1s 5d	12s 6d
30			£28 11s

John Pryce Morris with No 7 at the 1926 station. His story is told on Page 108. Aberystwyth station master Arthur E. Humphreys lodged with him in 1911.

CAMBRIAN RAILWAYS – PERSONNEL EMPLOYED ON NARROW GAUGE RAILWAYS

Locomotive department (RAIL92/142)
Aberystwyth

	Date of birth	Joined	Position	Wages/day	
Richard Humphreys Edwards	18 October 1895	15 March 1914	Fireman Vale of Rheidol Railway	5 May 1919 - 3s 8 August 1919 – 9s 6d 16 May 1921 – 10s 6d	On strike 26 September – 6 October 1919
John Edward Davies	22 November 1887	21 December 1902	Fireman Vale of Rheidol Railway	7 July 1914 – 3s 8d (4s 6d when driving) 18 August 1919 – 12s	On strike 26 September – 6 October 1919
Joseph Probert Salmon	12 November 1865	April 1907	Cleaner Vale of Rheidol Railway	3s	On strike 26 September – 6 October 1919
Edward Griffiths	2 December 1870	8 January 1912	Fitter Vale of Rheidol Railway	5s 8d 24 August 1916 – 6s	Died 15 August 1917
William Joseph Evans	13 June 1860	1 May 1902	Joiner Vale of Rheidol Railway	4s 1d	On strike 26 September – 6 October 1919
Henry Millman	20 January 1863	1 May 1902	Assistant Fitter Vale of Rheidol Railway	3s 6d	On strike 26 September – 6 October 1919 Died 25 December 1922
Evan Williams	31 May 1855	1 April 1870	Engineman Vale of Rheidol Railway	5s 4d - 2 December 1902	Left of own accord 12 December 1918

Employed by the Vale of Rheidol Railway from 22 December 1902, Evan Williams was the only engineman allocated exclusively to it by the Cambrian, which had sacked him on 4 November 1899 for passing a signal at danger at Talwrn Bach on 12 October, 'thereby causing fatal accident to Ganger [Edward] Humphreys'. Humphreys had been killed trying to close the level crossing gate when he realised that the train was not going to stop. (*Cambrian News* 20 October 1899)

DATA SUBMITTED TO THE LIGHT RAILWAYS INVESTIGATION COMMITTEE 1921

Goods traffic 1919	Tons
Grain	345
Groceries	101
Pit wood	4,560
Ale and porter	26
Manure	20
Basic slag	93
Bricks	31
Coal and coke	747
Lime	148
Spelter	244
Lead ore	42

	1913	1919
Engine mileage		
Coaching, loaded	25,210	12,840
Coaching, unloaded	91	-
Freight	13,421	13,252
Shunting		2,600
Total	38,722	28,693
Passengers	144,593	118,569
Goods (tons)	475	4,908
Minerals (tons)	1,853	497
Revenue		
Goods, &c	£701 4s 11d	£2,779 1s 5d
Passengers	£4,887	£7,092
The 1913 figures for goods and minerals do not correlate with the figures in the previous table		

Train staff	Summer months	1 guard, 4 drivers, 4 firemen, 2 cleaners
	Winter months	1 guard, 2 drivers, 2 firemen, 1 cleaner
Station staff		3 station masters, 4 porters, 1 goods porter at exchange siding
Maintenance staff		1 fitter and assistant, 1 joiner, 8 platelayers in two gangs and supervised by one of the main line inspectors
Part-time staff	Summer months	1 driver, 1 fireman

Accommodation at stations	
Aberystwyth	3 sidings and loop, accommodation for 25 wagons, goods yard accommodation
Exchange	accommodation for 12 wagons
Capel Bangor	2 sidings and loop, accommodation for 30 wagons, 1 siding into carriage shed
Devil's Bridge	2 sidings and loop, accommodation for 18 wagons, goods yard accommodation
No accommodation for dealing with livestock, van or carriage traffic.	

With No 1213 in the foreground, 1923-built summer cars in the trains and goods stock in the yard, this view of Devil's Bridge was a typical scene in the 1920s and '30s. (John Scott Morgan collection)

CAPITAL EXPENDITURE ON EXTENSION TO GENERAL STATION 1925-6

	Capital	Engineering	Signals	Telegraphs
Provision of loop to hold 7 coaches and van and necessary connection; crossover in station; fencing at each end of ramp; cattle guards at Smithfield Road	£753			
Substituted permanent way		£77		
Removal and refix buffer stops		£15		
Removal and refix shelter and station nameboards		£5		
Original cost of wall displaced in providing opening for platform gate		£18		
Signals			£75	
Telegraphs				£25
Raising level of land by tipping		£750		
Contract with Jones Bros for filling gardens	£300			
Additional expenditure due to extension of departure line and provision of gates at Smithfield Road	£130			

RESULTS FOR 1924/5

	Expenditure		Receipts					
Traffic department staff	1924	1925	1924	1925	Passengers	Parcels	Goods	Total
Aberystwyth	£434	£886	£4,745		£4,114	£39	£992	
Devil's Bridge	£210	£362	£955		£308	£10		£5,463
Summer staff	£282	-						
	£926	£1,248						
Loco department, engine and train running expenses – passenger		£3,757						
Freight		£766						
Engineering department, maintenance and renewal		£2,215						
Signal department		£187						
Clothing		£14						
Fuel, lighting, water and general stores		£5						
Rates		£226						
		£8,414						

Wagons in the yard at Devil's Bridge in the 1920s. (John Scott Morgan collection)

APPENDIX 12

ESTIMATE OF OPERATING COSTS 1961

Train movement costs			
Provision, renewal, interest and maintenance of engines and coaches		£3,634	
Running costs – engines and coaches		£1,348	
Trainmen		£1,426	£6,408
Station costs			
Staff – no basis of apportionment available			
Building maintenance – branch stations only		£8	£8
Track and signalling			
Permanent way gang wages and materials		£953	
Track relaying proportion		£154	
Bridge, fences, cabins, etc maintenance and renewal (proportion)		£213	
		£1,320	
Signalling staff costs	£723		
Maintenance and renewal (proportion) of facilities	£121		
Rental of GPO telephone line	£184	£1,028	£2,348
Publicity			£394
			£9,158

APPENDIX 13

VALUATION OF VALE OF RHEIDOL LIGHT RAILWAY, DECEMBER 1962

Land	£36,000
Permanent way, buildings, bridges, fences, level crossings, culverts, drains, etc (in situ)	£32,750
Signalling and telecommunications equipment	£390
Rolling stock	£3,660
	£72,800

VALUATION OF ROLLING STOCK, 30 NOVEMBER 1962

	Type	Quantity	Year built	Book life	Original cost	Gross replacement cost	Residual value
Locomotives							
No 9	2-6-2T	1	1902	50 years	£1,750	£10,750	£390
No 7	2-6-2T	1	1923	50 years	£2,737	£10,750	£390
No 8	2-6-2T	1	1923	50 years	£2,737	£10,750	£390
Coaching stock							
	Non-gangwayed corridor 2nd	4	1923	40 years	£2,604	£8,050	£520
	Non-gangwayed corridor 2nd	10	1938	40 years	£4,790	£15,700	£1,300
	Non-gangwayed open 2nd brake	2	1938	40 years	£990	£3,250	£260
	Luggage and brake	3	1938	40 years	£678	£2,340	£260
Freight vehicles							
	Mineral wagons	4	1904	25 years	£168	£1,120	£60
Service vehicles							
	Ballast wagons	4	1904	35 years	£108	£720	£60
	Rail wagons	2	1904	40 years	£84	£560	£30
					£16,646	£63,990	£3,660
Conversions							
	Flats (stores and material)	2					£30

ESTIMATED OUTLAY FOR RE-ROUTING VALE OF RHEIDOL LINE INTO MAIN STATION

	Original	Revised
Track alterations, loco facilities, platforms	£2,950	£5,020
Signalling	£948	£2,378
Shell Mex & BP pipe line	£1,650	£1,831
	£5,540	£9,229

A view of the east end of the loco shed as seen in the 1990s. The oil depot that required a temporary pipeline to be built across the railway is on the right.

EXPLANATION OF OVERSPENDING ON RE-LOCATION WORKS 1968

Signalling and telegraphs		
Amount underestimated for original work	£357	
Additional signalling not originally taken into account down refuge siding	£1,081	£1,438
Civil engineering		
New sleepers and track not originally allowed for	£200	
Tarmac road surface, underestimated	£25	
Additional labour costs	£127	
Widening internal pit (estimate)	£200	
Repair to transfer siding for passenger train operation during first week, £75 plus overheads, cost over recovering 846 yards of plain line and 110 yards of crossing work. Only 400 yards allowed for in original estimate.	£583	
Consequent loss of credit	£275	£1,410
Shell Mex & BP		
Original amount authorised	£1,650	
First account	£1,275	
Final account	£556	
	£1,831	
Overspending		£181
Additional work		
Civil engineering		
Internal pit to be deepened from 2ft to 3ft	£50	
Internal pit rail support wall to be replaced by piers with 4ft centres (£390) and external ashpit to be lengthened to 10ft between rails and on the side (£140)	£530	
Track alterations inside shed to permit stabling of coach sets and coaling of locos beyond the shed. Will allow coal wagons to be recovered.	£80	
		£660
Total		£3,689

STAFF EMPLOYED ON VALE OF RHEIDOL RAILWAY 1968

Position	Wages	Overtime	Sunday duty	Bonus	Consequence of sale
Drivers (2)	£1,096	£140	£74	£74	Redundant – difficult to place for 38 weeks per annum
Secondmen (2)	£806	£110	£60		Ditto
Shedman	£175	£49	£63		Ditto
Fitter	£195	£137	£84		Ditto
Guards (2)	£474	£65	£69	£30	Deployed elsewhere, would lose overtime
Carriage & wagon examiner			£36		Deployed elsewhere, would lose overtime
Signalman			£78		Would lose Sunday overtime
Station foreman			£68		Would lose Sunday overtime
Porter			£61		Would lose Sunday overtime
Clerk			£84		Would lose Sunday overtime
Carriage serviceman and porter *	£336			£42	Would not be re-engaged
Wages under these heads totalled £4,401. Employment costs totalling £1,270 were incurred by the civil and signalling engineers for maintenance. * temporary summer staff					

The historian C.C. Green was a great enthusiast for the Vale of Rheidol Railway, taking thousands of photographs of the railway and its rolling stock. This is his photograph of 1938-built saloon No W4145 at Aberystwyth in June 1954. (C.C. Green/Michael Bishop collection)

OPERATING COSTS 1986

8 footplate/guards		
2 seasonal staff		
50% one clerk		£67,000
Locomotive costs		
5 staff	£43,000	
Materials	£10,000	
Fuel	£25,000	£78,000
Civil engineering costs		£85,000
Publicity		£10,000
Total		£240,000
The area manager Shrewsbury thought that he could eliminate a traffic manager's post without the Vale of Rheidol Railway. Costs could be reduced by increasing staff productivity and eliminating restrictive practices.		

Few enthusiasts visit the railway's halts. This view of Glanrafon dates from the 1960s.

TICKETS SOLD 1958-87, 1989-2016

	Tickets sold	Passenger journeys
1958	25,894	
1959	29,559	
1960	31,384	
1961	26,667	
1962	26,420	
1963	34,560	
1964	40,365	
1965	42,808	
1966	46,471	
1967	46,301	
1968	48,532	
1969	52,090	95,459
1970	62,241	117,722
1971	69,317	128,278
1972	76,680	142,501
1973	89,131	167,549
1974	92,369	172,714
1975	96,334	179,200
1976	85,668	155,400
1977	86,559	160,480
1978	84,842	
1979	72,481	
1980	60,752	
1981	59,412	
1982	55,700	
1983	55,100	
1984	58,400	
1985	52,700	
1986	50,300	
1987	51,000	

	Tickets sold
1989	44,294
1990	43,601
1991	41,209
1992	31,866
1993	34,397
1994	33,278
1995	35,925
1996	36,389
1997	37,568
1998	34,501
1999	34,555
2000	31,854
2001	31,200
2002	34,058
2003	38,753
2004	38,032
2005	36,318
2006	34,580
2007	35,732
2008	35,232
2009	38,763
2010	40,657
2011	41,319
2012	40,273
2013	43,703
2014	48,657
2015	50,194
2016	55,648

1958-87 data extracted from BR files at the National Archives, 1989-2016 data provided by the Vale of Rheidol Railway.

WORK CARRIED OUT BY THE BRECON MOUNTAIN RAILWAY AT BR EXPENSE 1989

Coaching stock		
2	Carriages to have repairs and repainting completed	
12	Carriages to be fettled up and repaired as needed	
12	Wheelsets to be fitted after reprofiling and brake gear to be reassembled	
4	Bogies to be exchanged	
	All remaining wheelsets to be examined and changed as needed	
	Labour and materials	£10,900
Locomotives		
No 8 to have repairs completed including rebushing and remetalling of motion, reriveting of front frame and pony truck stretchers, repairs to bunkers and tanks, adjustments to axle centres running out of true, attention to pipework and fuel leaks, fitting refractory material to firebox and completion of boiler inspection. Labour and materials		£3,200
No 9 to have repairs completed including refitting tube plate, stays, tubes and smokebox, refitting and repairs to tanks and bunkers, rebushing and remetalling of motion. Repairs to pony trucks. Strip and repair boiler fittings, remetalling of axle boxes, fitting retyred wheelsets and re-erection of locomotive and boiler inspection. Labour and materials		£8,900
		£23,000

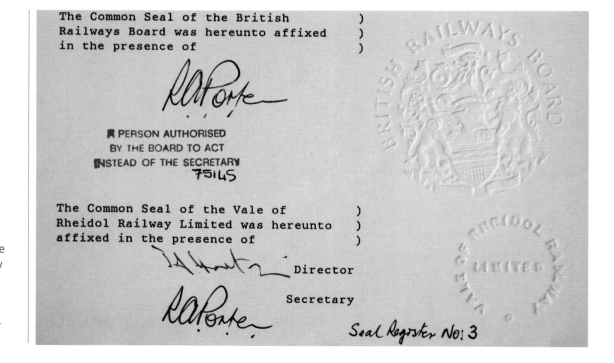

The Common Seal of the British)
Railways Board was hereunto affixed)
in the presence of)

R PERSON AUTHORISED
BY THE BOARD TO ACT
INSTEAD OF THE SECRETARY
75145

The Common Seal of the Vale of)
Rheidol Railway Limited was hereunto)
affixed in the presence of)

Director

Secretary

Seal Register No: 3

The seals of the British Railways Board and the Vale of Rheidol Railway Ltd applied to the application for the light railway amendment order in 1988.

PLANNING APPLICATIONS

22 August 1983	Devil's Bridge	Retention of portacabin to provide buffet	Temporary
17 June 1986	Devil's Bridge	Renewal of permission for portacabin to provide buffet	
21 March 1989	Aberystwyth	Provision of temporary booking office and information point	Temporary
21 March 1989	Devil's Bridge	Refurbishment and extension of existing station to include cafe, toilets, shop and booking office	Refused
21 April 1989	Devil's Bridge	Extension to existing building to provide shop, cafe and larger toilets	Listed building consent – refused
25 April 1990	Devil's Bridge	Renewal of permission for portacabin to provide cafe at station	
15 August 1990	Aberystwyth	Provision of temporary booking office and information point for passengers (Renewal)	Temporary
27 March 1991	Llanbadarn	Replacement of existing railway bridge	
26 January 1994	Devil's Bridge	Temporary siting of portacabin tea bar for railway passengers	Temporary
26 January 1994	Aberystwyth	Temporary siting of booking office and information point for Vale of Rheidol Railway Passengers	
16 March 1999	Devil's Bridge	Renewal of temporary permission for cafe	Temporary
11 April 2002	Aberystwyth	Change of use from disused cattle market to new car park for Vale of Rheidol Railway	
4 March 2003	Aberystwyth	Retention of temporary building for booking office	Temporary
28 May 2008	Aberystwyth	Erection of running and maintenance shed for use in connection with the movement of traffic	Certificate of lawful development
16 August 2017	Devil's Bridge	Change of use of amenity land to car parking	Certificate of lawful development – refused
9 March 2018	Devil's Bridge	Provision of new car parking area	

BIBLIOGRAPHY

Boyd, J.I.C.; *Narrow Gauge Railways in Mid-Wales*; Oakwood Press, 2nd edition, 1970

Chater, A.O.; Inscriptions on bridges in Cardigan; *Ceredigion*, Journal of the Cardiganshire Antiquarian Society, 1979 Vol 8 No 3

Cozens, Lewis; *The Vale of Rheidol Railway*; Author, 1950

Cozens, Lewis; *The Plynlimon & Hafan Tramway*; Author, 1955

Fenton, R.S.; *Cambrian Coasters – steam and motor coaster owners of North and West Wales*; World Ship Society, 1989

Gardner, Richard; Rheidol Incident; *Railway World*, September 1986

Gasquoine, C.P.; *The Story of the Cambrian – a biography of a railway*; Woodall, Minshall, Thomas & Co, 1922

Green, C.C.; *The Coast Lines of the Cambrian Railways Volume 1*; Wild Swan, 1993

Green, C.C.; *The Vale of Rheidol Light Railway*; Wild Swan, 1986

de Havilland, John; *Industrial Locomotives of Dyfed & Powys*; Industrial Railway Society, 1994

Hopwood, H.L.; The Vale of Rheidol Line (Cambrian Railways); *Railway Magazine*, June 1921

Johnson, Peter; *The Cambrian Railways – a new history*; Oxford Publishing Co, 2013

Lazard Brothers & Company; *Vale of Rheidol Railway Limited – invitation to tender*; Lazard Brothers & Company, 1988

Macfarlane, Harold; The Vale of Rheidol Light Railway; *Railway Magazine*, September 1903

Metcalfe, Richard; *Davies & Metcalfe Ltd Railway Engineers to the World*; Senior Publications/Foxline Publications, 1999

Oxley, J. Stewart; *Light Railways Procedure*; Jordan & Sons/W. Hay Fielding, 1901

Rees, James; The Romance of the Vale of Rheidol Railway; unpublished paper, 1943 (donated to W.E. Hayward and preserved in the WEH-lyn Collection at the National Archives, ZSPC11/640)

Wade, E.A.; *The Plynlimon & Hafan Tramway*; Twelveheads Press, 2nd edition, 1997

INDEX